glottal stop

WESLEYAN POETRY

glottal stop

101 poems by

paul celan

TRANSLATED BY

Nikolai Popov & Heather McHugh

WESLEYAN UNIVERSITY PRESS

Published by University Press of New England

Hanover & London

WESLEYAN UNIVERSITY PRESS
Published by University Press of New England,
Hanover, NH 03755
Front matter, notes, and English translations
© 2000 by Nikolai Popov and Heather McHugh
All rights reserved
Printed in United States of America
5 4 3 2 1
CIP data appear at the end of the book

The poems translated in this book (with the
exception of "Don't sign your name" / "*Schreib dich
nicht*") were collected in Paul Celan, *Gesammelte
Werke* © Suhrkamp Verlag, 1983 (see Index for
volume and page). They were originally published in
German in the following works and are translated
herein by permission of the publishers:

Works by Paul Celan copyrighted by Suhrkamp
Verlag Frankfurt am Main: *Atemwende*, © 1967;
Fadensonnen, © 1968; *Lichtzwang*, © 1970;
Schneepart, © 1971; *Zeitgehoft*, © 1976;
Eingedunkelt, © 1983.

Paul Celan, "Stimmen," "Sommerbericht," taken
from *Sprachgitter*, © S. Fischer Verlag, Frankfurt am
Main, 1959. "Bei Wein und Verlorenheit," "Selbdritt,
Selbviert," "Erratisch," "Einiges Handähnliche,"
"Einem, der vor der Tür stand," "Ein Wurfholz,"
"Wohin mir das Wort" "Die Silbe Schmerz," and "La
Contrescarpe," taken from *Die Niemandsrose*, ©
S. Fischer Verlag, Frankfurt am Main, 1963.

UK and Commonwealth rights to publish a new
translation of "Bei Wein und Verlorenheit" by Paul
Celan are granted by Anvil Press Poetry Ltd.

CONTENTS

ACKNOWLEDGMENTS

Our enterprise benefited from the generosity of many friends and colleagues. Jerry Glenn read an early version of the manuscript and made invaluable comments; over the years we were encouraged and supported by James Lyon, John Felstiner, Robert Pinsky, John Hollander, Michael Speier, and the late Ernst Behler. Our editors at Wesleyan University Press—Suzanna Tamminen and Tom Radko—kept the faith through a protracted copyright negotiation. Sarah Spence at Literary Imagination, by contacting Petra Hardt at SuhrkampVerlag, enabled us to break the copyright ice-jam. Yehuda Amichai blessed our very first efforts. We thank them all.

The following magazines originally published or reprinted (sometimes under other titles) poems now collected here:

Boston Review
   With wine and being lost, with
   Threesome, Foursome
   Frankfurt, September
   Your heart manholed
The Drunken Boat
   Who
   Lyon, Les Archers
   Eternity gets older: at
Harper's
   Come, we are cutting out
   Windfield bound for winter: this
   Weather hand
   Open glottis, air flow
   The cables have already been laid
Jubilat
   Floated down blackwater rapids
   Spasms, I love you, psalms

Graygreens
Ring-narrowing Day, under
Attached to out-cast
Chitin sunlings
Literary Imagination
The sight of the songbirds
Gigantic
Come, we are cutting out
Windfield bound for winter: this
Weather hand
Open glottis, air flow
The cables have already been laid
Marlboro Review
Voices, scored into
Noisemakers shoot into the Light: it's the Truth
As loud colors, heaped up
White, white, white
Haut Mal
Seneca Review
Coincidence staged, the signs all
Eyeshot's island, broken
Flung wood
You with the dark slingshot
Out of angel flesh, on
Pain, the syllable
Verse
Erratic
Gray-white of sheer
At high noon, in
Go back and add up
Half-mauled, mask
Wet from the world
Hush, you hag, and ferry me across the rapids
Walls of speech, inwards space
She of the freckled farewells
And force and pain

In 1992 when we began this project, our intention was to supply versions of Celan poems not yet available in English.[1] Such a restriction focused our attention on Celan's collections *Fadensonnen* and *Atemwende*. As our work progressed we added untranslated poems from Celan's later books and retranslated a few poems already available in English, for the sake of contextual coherence (Celan's later poems often quote, allude to, or rewrite earlier poems of his). We believe that only a wide *range* of translatorial approaches can do justice to a poetry as complex as Celan's, and through our selection and method we have emphasized some of his understudied poetic virtues. Our selection bypasses many major poems of Celan's middle period (most of those can be found in Neugroschel and Hamburger); it contains poems from a later, less known, and more opaque, elusive, or downright disturbing body of work. We hope that our selection will surprise readers—those familiar with former translations and those about to encounter Celan for the first time—as we ourselves were surprised by the range of Celan's imagination, by the variety of poems he was capable of writing in his last decade, and by the exquisite formal discipline of those poems (written at a time of profound personal crisis).

Out of respect for Celan's aesthetic control and integrity, we restricted ourselves to poems for which we could find, in English, sufficiently rich or opportune poetic resources to justify publication. No one can reproduce in a language other than German Celan's tragic relation to the language which was his instrument and life, a language that had remained silent through the horror. Like Büchner's, his words come to us framed by those invisible quotation marks that always listen "not without fear, for something beyond themselves,

1. We had in mind such creditable collections as those published by Michael Hamburger, Joachim Neugroschel, Katharine Washburn and Margret Guillemin, and Brian Lynch and Peter Jankowsky, as well as John Felstiner's translations and reflections on translating Celan.

beyond words."[2] The beauty, the daring, and the tragedy of Celan's poetry cannot be comprehended merely in terms of reference. (What is "reference" in Celan?) We sought, cautiously, to create poems that follow Celan's intentional mode (Benjamin's *Art des Meinens*), and the intensity of his listening to language itself. Given the fundamentals of Celan's poetics (phono-graphic, grammatical, and rhetorical), any attempt to isolate a "literal" meaning apart from those fundamentals would seriously impoverish and distort the effect of the poems, both individually and as a whole. Everything in a poem is literal, that is, made of letters, blanks, and their interrelationships on the page, and the literal is everything. Precisely this omnipresence of the letter, and the depth of Celan's probings into the matrix of his "original" language, prohibit naive replications of line or meaning. Celan's word order in German is quite natural, but the same linear order in English can sometimes misleadingly suggest experiments in syntax where there are none, and so drown out other features of his formal daring. In short, we often sought higher levels of fidelity than those of the word, the line, or the individual poem: Working on a fairly large body of poems allowed us to re-create, where possible in English, effects that seemed characteristic of his art as a whole, for example, Celan's frequent use of paronymy not as an embellishing but as a *structuring* device, or his way of wrenching a word apart so that its parts would speak as loudly as the whole.

In the course of our sift, we threw out about a third of the approximately one hundred and fifty poems translated in all—precisely in the cases where we felt we had not advanced significantly beyond a working version of mere meaning. The admirability of a poem in its original German was a necessary but not a sufficient raison d'être for its final inclusion in this book; its conduciveness to the resources of English poetry had to meet a very high standard, too. In other words, we required of ourselves extraordinary results in the target language: Nothing short of that selectiveness seemed sufficient homage to Celan himself.

2. Paul Celan, "The Meridian: Speech on the Occasion of Receiving the Georg Büchner Prize, Darmstadt, 22 October 1960," tr. R. Waldrop.

Because first and foremost we value the experience of the poetry, we decided not to print the German texts en face. Both of us were reluctant to encourage, in the process of fostering an international readership's acquaintance with Paul Celan, too early a recourse to the kind of line-by-line comparison that fatally distracts attention from what matters first: the experience of a poem's coursing, cumulative power. The serious scholar will have no trouble looking up the poetic originals; the serious reader will have no objection to focusing on a poem's presence and integrity. Neither the one nor the other will ever forget that, no matter how plausible a poem may sound in its target language, it remains a poem *in translation*, an encounter marked by surprise, ambiguity, affection, and violence.

*   *   *

As a mysterious paradigm of the encounter between self and other, the process of translation itself suggested the title for our enterprise. The glottis is not a thing but an interstice: the space between vocal chords. A glottal stop is, in Webster's words, "the speech sound produced by momentary complete closure of the glottis, followed by explosive release." Celan uses the term to end the poem "Frankfurt, September": "the glottal stop is breaking into song." In this poem, each of a series of obstructions gives way to a version of expression: blindness to brilliance, flat rasters to 3-D sweat, lamentations to open-mindedness, glottal stop to song. (One could say that the arc described in the latter instance is that from linguistic precision to poetic uncontainability.) Celan's poetry abounds in motifs of the mother's death in a concentration camp: she died of a wound to the throat. If utterances issue from a gaping hole, so too does blood: the place of vulnerability is also the place of poetry.

         *   *   *
What need of Day—
To those whose Dark—hath so—surpassing Sun—
It deem it be—continually—
At the Meridian?

    Emily Dickinson (#611)

Paul Celan's own translations of Emily Dickinson are astonishingly post-emptive: Dickinson is the star he starts from, not the one he's shooting for. Like Dickinson's, his own is a work of opportune attenuations—famously obscure, and famously oversimplifiable. Its polysemies arise from architectonic terseness. To replicate such arts in English, we had to bring to the occasion two quite separate sensibilities. The partnership of a European-born literary scholar-exegete and an American poet and translator brought, we believe, unusual range and resource to the enterprise. Having worked together on Celan translations now for half of our married life, we are not insensible of its status in (and perhaps as) the matrimonial tragicomedy. For where Celan combines traits of scholar and poet in a single figure, we divvy it up, or duke it out. It is in the nature of translation that it should provide a most congenial medium for contrary cooperation.[3] In the course of our Celanian struggles we found out how often the logomania of the one was at war with the logician's nature in the other. Effects one found diabolical the other found divine; foundings the one divined, the other bedeviled. Where one's headlights were trained for clarification, the other loved the half-lights. If one read first and foremost through the lens of intellectual history and literary precedent, the other was big on immediacy's intricacies, the patterns of rhetoric, rhetorics of image: parallels, counterpoises, serial effects. Our dispositions did some chiastic entwining: The poet's analytical acuity balanced and corrected the scholar's verbal high jinks (haunted by his memory of having once been a translator of James Joyce). We were of several

3. As John Felstiner puts it, "in translating, as in parody, critical and creative activity converge. The fullest reading of a poem gets realized moment by moment in the writing of a poem. So translation presents not merely a paradigm but the utmost case of engaged literary interpretation."

minds; we were consoled to know that so too was Celan. Ultimately the domestic battles between reason and what *la raison ne connait pas* were representative of his own psychomachies: Celan wrestles with angels of both realms.

But his premises are never merely dualistic. They comprehend desert and open ocean, glacier and swamp—inhospitable landscapes that exert peculiar pressures on the human visitor. Celan can make earth itself seem an alien place. And just wait till you see Celanian space: The poems are uncommonly satel-lit, mother-shipped, moon-probed, tele-commed. His eye is alert to its own instruments (like Spinoza, he sees the world through the structure of a tear) and his views assume a global curve. Passing whether across philosophy or physics, theology or military logistics, his eye takes due note of the sensual details, zooming from electron microscopy's expanses all the way to the intimacies of interplanetary camerawork; from the closest big dark cells of politics or sex, all the way to the soul's own smallest far-flung star.

Among the jargons at his casual disposal are those of jurisprudence and geology, anatomy and neurophysiology, nautical and aeronautical navigations, heavy industry and manufacturing, biotech and electronics, cabbalistic esoterica, philological finesses. You can find, in these poetic reliquaries, such odd bedfellows as karst and carpel, korbel and syncope, saxifrages and sporangia, raised bogs and swan ponds. There are brain mantles, nerve cells, auditory canals, X-rays. There are conveyor belts and pressurized helmets, mine shafts and shower rooms. Lines of communication are bundled with tricks of synapse; mainstays can't be untied; brain-waves are made in rain-pools. Celan has a lot of gray matter in his hold, and he's bailing like mad. (Surely he understood Beckett's definition of tears as "liquefied brain.")

For all the otherworldliness of these poems, there's a distinctively Celanian atmosphere. Ominous with flashing and floating signs, ashen words and sinking letters, numerals blown about in wind, it sometimes seems a domain of gamblers, Kabbalists, palm-readers, jugglers and tightrope walkers: domain of oddities and omens. There are whiffs of the famously biographical topoi of the camps (the gas and shower facilities, the dishes of the dead); evocations of his murdered mother, severance at every throat and windpipe. It would be easy for a biographizing sensibility to read his literary aporias into only that connection. But all is not so easily stylizable: consider, for example, the fierce array of female figures in the poems, especially of the darker muses: venomous vamps, festering fecundities. (Among the features of a Celanian carnality are its undermined grounds—or underground mind: The roots of the sexual seem to be set in moist mephitic places for which the poet feels, as often as not, an undisguised disgust. Look at the corrupted love song he calls "Haut Mal"—in which he apostrophizes his black-tongued, foul-mouthed, all-but-coprophagic mate. It's a poem that begins in soot and sex, and ends in sacrilege. It's so illicit it's delicious.) Words may be "dirty" precisely because of the mud in man's mouth: Man is a creature of soil, whether proceeding from dust to dust—or from the lightning bolt to the puddle.

Having relegated the hermeneutic particulars of allusion and side-reading to our notes (at the back of the book), we'll mention here only a few of the force-fields in Celan-land that from the very first attracted our explorer-instincts, the ones that made Celanian realms seem crucial to a reader today. (Already in mid-century Celan was seeding the poems with millennial references. Like Dickinson, perhaps he sensed the proleptic nature of the work a brilliant poetry performs, creating a readership the poet will not live to see.) Celan himself refers to his work as a kind of "spectral analysis"—a scientific term that does not for a moment diminish the mysteries of its application to (and as) poetry. It is a peculiar sort of sensory materialization one finds in lines like these: "white, white, white, / like paint on pickets / the laws line up / and march right in." (In German the word "white" is only a whisper away from the first-person present form of the verb "know," thus from the shades of gray matter.) In another poem, gray-greenishness is "dug out" from a well—a characteristic materialization of the search for something beyond the evidentiary surfaces. If Celan's a spiritual seeker, he's doing it with dredges, shovels, mining equipment, scoops, claws, and light-probes, examining body and mind for physical evidence of God, to materialize whose name would be idolatry. Elsewhere emotions are gouged from a landscape as nominalized color ("gray-white of sheer / excavated feeling"). It's the mind that does the feeling. The hand is all eyes.

At times, the landscapes of man and mind and language seem synonymous. The remarkers may be moved, the markers may float (even continents and anchors shift; there are forms of tug and barge for moving meaning), but at the bottom of it all, past the shells and slimes of ultimate (or originary things), there's something unspeakable.

Sometimes the Celanian pool is a stone-gray surface (across which felt and faithful swans may steer their way). On one poem's stone surface appears lettering, beneath which Celan imagines a "deep brother-letter," to put us in several minds at once: of lapidary inscription's role in human memory, and also of the prospective (and projective) force of language itself, making its attempts on the timeless. From the surface folds or levees of the stream of consciousness, we should not then be surprised to find ourselves fallen into the fossae (or ditches) of the brain, where anatomical nomenclature places the "calamus scriptorius"—near the center that controls breath: These are characteristic Celanian premises: the stone in the head, the stab-wound in the throat, words that hurt. *Stich*[4] is stab in German, but it means a line of verse in Russian (Celan jocoseriously referred to himself as a Russian poet in the realm of German infidels). In German, the word for letter (the letter of a word) is *Buchstab* (book-staff). The Runic sticks and stones that hurtle across these networks of etymology and morphology are dear, in every sense, to a Celanian temperament: As a poet-philosopher, he suffers the materiality of language; as a son and husband and father, he suffers the dematerializations of love. Through the polyglot exile's several homes (German, Rumanian, Russian, French, and English) wander many ghost-guests and gists. They amount to a memory, and morphology, of meaning.

Even in the strictest technical vocabularies he frequents, Celan favors those concerned with seeing things through, or seeing through them: He is attracted to the lensgrinder's craft (perhaps because of Spinoza), and to the realms of X-ray technicians (a ghostly science if ever there was one). What happens to the metaphysician after Dachau is a famous question. What happens to the physician

---

4. From the Greek *stikhos*; hence "distich" and other prosodic terms of Greek origin.

after Mengele is not so often asked. But it is that question that drives the closer to the heart of Celan's excruciations. He's a serious sensualist, in whose hands spirit's question must be retooled for ever more exquisite senses of sense, ever more painful instrumentalities. However fundamentally mental may be Celan's vertiginous moves across space and time, he's never any the less fascinated by the material markers of the moved mind: its Doppler effects and red shifts. Suffering has a cerebral cortex; the grim reaper sports a brain mantle. *Grau* means gray, in German; but *Grauen* means horror.

"Acephalic by choice" he calls the Thou-less tribe. His outcry is of inwit, a nightmare's EEG. God's rod and staff, far from being a comfort, are rather (like retinal structures and letter-formations) made to make us see: see with the mind's eye, if no other—the same eye, says Meister Eckhart, through which God sees us. The infinite sands come to be ground through the hourglass; where time is contained, it also runs out. The watch-crystal gives its name to a form of quaking bog; the message in the bottle is stoppered; the wind-rose (a compass at sea) is disoriented. Under glass, the eye looks back: It sees that it cannot see. "Right away, / the teardrop took shape—." "Your destination the one / precise crystal."

Paul Celan died by drowning. He did it not just reflexively, but transitively: He died by drowning himself. As figures of flotation and immersion recur throughout the poems, particularly those that refer to writing, it is natural that—like so much else in the Celanian legend—those figures come to seem fatefully proleptic. (As subjects and objects of our own regards, readers and writers of our own lives, we hold out as long as we can—like "dreamproof tugs—each / with a vulture-claw / towing a part / of the still- /unsunken sign.") Paul Celan's attraction for readers today may be deeply ideogrammatical: He made himself a glancing stroke, a winking wave, withdrawal's sign. As waters rise toward iris-level, as the eye-globe is covered, a greatening force of mind informs the sensual field. In the face of grief, in the light of death, in the vale of tears, what does intellect do? Of sinking things, thinking sings.

H M, N P
Seattle, 1999

glottal stop

Voices, scored into
the waters' green.
When the kingfisher dives,
the split second whirs:

What stood by you
appears on every shore
mown down
into another image.

*   *   *

Voices from the nettles:

Come to us on your hands.
All you can read, alone
with a lamp, is your palm.

*   *   *

Voices, night-knotted, ropes
on which you hang your bell.

Dome yourself over, world:
when death's shell washes up on shore
a bell will want to ring.

*   *   *

Voices that make your heart
recoil into your mother's.
Voices from the hanging-tree
where old growth and young growth
exchange rings.

*   *   *

Voices, guttural, amid the debris,
where even infinity shovels,
runnels of
(cardio-) slime.

Launch here the boats I manned,
my son.

Amidships, when an evil wind takes charge,
the clamps and brackets close.

Jacob's voice:

The tears.
Tears in the eye of my brother.
One clung. It grew.
We live in there.
Now, breathe—
so it may
fall.

*   *   *

Voices inside the ark:

Only
the mouths
were saved. Hear us,
o sinking things.

*   *   *

No
voice–
late noise, stranger to the hour,
gift to your thoughts, born of
wakefulness here in the final
account: a
carpel, large as an eye, and deeply
scored: bleeds
sap, and won't
heal over.

Summer Report

No longer crossed, the carpet of thyme
is bypassed instead.
A blank line beaten
through the heather.
No windfall in the storm swath.

Encounters once again with
scattered words, like
riprap, scrubgrass, time.

With wine and being lost, with
less and less of both:

I rode through the snow, do you read me,
I rode God far—I rode God
near, he sang,
it was
our last ride over
the hurdled humans.

They cowered when
they heard us
overhead, they
wrote, they
lied our neighing
into one of their
image-ridden languages.

Threesome, Foursome

In the dooryard, puckered mint,
you pucker back, you leaf a hint.

Mind this hour, it is your time,
mine the mouth and yours the rhyme.

Mine's the mouth, though it is still,
full of words that will not fill.

Some spell narrowness, some breadth,
all recall the brush with death.

I make one, and we make three,
one half bound, one half free.

In the dooryard, puckered mint,
you pucker back, you leave a hint.

Erratic

Evenings delve
into your eye. Lip-
picked syllables—
a lovely voiceless circle—
help the creeping star
into their ring. The stone, once
close to the temporal zones, now opens up:

my soul, you were
in the ether with all
the other
scattershot suns.

Hand-
like, shadowy,
it showed up with
the blades of grass:

right away—downheartedness, you
potter!—the hour provided
clay, right away
the teardrop took shape:—

then once again it hemmed us in
with its panicle of blue, this new
today.

To one who stood outside the door, one
evening:
to him
I opened my word—: off to
the ugly changeling he trudged, I saw him, to the
mis-
begotten one, to the brother
born in a muddy mercenary's
boot, to the
twittering homunculus
with God's bloody
phallus.

Rebbe, I gnashed my teeth, Rebbe
Loew:

cise
this one's
word, write
the living
nothing-
ness into
this one's
heart, spread
this one's
two crippled fingers into a healer's
benediction.
This one's.

. . . .

And Rebbe, slam shut evening's door.

. . . .

Rip open morning's, Re—

Flung wood
on the windpipe's path,
so it goes, wing-
powered,
true,
taking off
along star-trails, kissed
by world-
shards, scarred
by time-
grains, time-dust,
your orphan sibling, lapilli, turned
dwarf, turned tiny, turned
to nothing,
gone away and done away, self-
rhyme—
and so it comes
back home,
in its turn re-
turns, to
hover on
a heartbeat, one
millennium, the only
hand on the dial
that one
soul—its own soul—
described, that
one
soul numbers
now.

How low could it go, my once-immortal word—
falling into the sky-pit right inside my skull,
the starflower now abides with me
accompanied there by spit and muck.

Rhymes in the night-house, breath in the dreck,
eye a slave to images—
and yet: staunch silence, rock
that vaults the very Devil's Stairway.

Pain, the Syllable

It gave itself into your hand:
a You, deathless,
where all self encountered itself. There was
a vortex of voices without words, empty forms,
and all went into them, mixed,
unmixed and
mixed again.

And numbers were
interwoven with the
Innumerable. A one, a thousand and what
before and after
was larger than itself,
and smaller, and full-
blown, and turning
back and forth into
the germinating Never.

Forgotten things
grasped at things to be forgotten,
earthparts, heartparts
swam,
they sank and swam. Columbus,
mind-
ful of the immortelle, the mother-
flower,
murdered mast and sail. And all put out to sea,

exploratory,
free,
and the wind-rose faded, shed
its leaves, and an ocean
flowered into shape and sight, in the blacklight
of a compass gone berserk. In coffins,
urns, canopies
the children woke up—
Jasper, Agate and Amethyst—nations,
tribes and kinfolk, a blind

LET THERE BE

tied itself into
the snakeheaded free-
coil—: a knot
(a counter knot, anti-knot, tauto-knot, double knot, and thou-
sand knot) at which the deep's
carnival-eyed litter
of star-martens,
letter by letter,
nib-, nib-, nib-
bled.

La Contrescarpe

Break the coin of breath
from the air around you and the tree:

anyone
hope
trundles up and down
Heart-Hump Road
must pay this toll—any-
one

at the turning-point
where he faces the spike of bread
that has drunk up the wine of his night, misery's
wine, wine of the king's
wakefulness.

Didn't the hands come along, holding their vigil,
and the happiness
deep in their cup,
didn't it come?
Didn't the March-pipe,
ciliated, come
with human sound that let there be light
at that time, from afar?

Did the dove go astray, could her ankle-band
be deciphered? (All the
clouding around her—it was legible.) Did the
covey countenance it? Did they understand,
and fly, when she did not return?

Roof-pitched slipway—that which floats
is laid down in dove-keel. The message bleeds
through the bulkheads,
every expiry
goes overboard too soon:

      Upon arrival in Berlin,
      via Krakow,
      you were met at the station by a plume of smoke,
      tomorrow's smoke already. Under
      the Paulownia trees
      you saw the knives erect, again,
      sharpened by distance. There was
      dancing. (*Quatorze
      juillets. Et plus de neuf autres.*)
      Cross Cut, Copy Cat, and Ugly Mug
      mimed your experiences. Wrapped
      in a banner, the Lord
      appeared to the flock. He took
      a pretty little sou-
      venir: a snapshot.
      The auto-
      release, that was
      you.

O this friend-
making. And yet, again,
you know your destination—the one
precise
crystal.

Floated down blackwater rapids,
past the sheen of
scars, are
forty trees of life,

completely stripped.
Upstream swimmer, woman, you alone
number them each, you touch them all.

Gray-white of sheer
excavated
feeling.

Beach-grasses scattered
here inland
blow sand patterns over
the smoke of wellside songs.

An ear, cut off, is listening.

An eye, cut into strips,
does justice to it all.

(I know you: you're the one who's bent so low.
You hold me—I'm the riddled one—in bondage.
What word could burn as witness for us two?
You're my reality. I'm your mirage.)

Singable remainder—trace
of one who—mute,
remote—broke out of bounds
through sicklescripts of snow.

Headed for the residue of a gaze
revolving under comet-
brows,
a tiny darkened heartmoon
packs the spark it caught
at large.

—Foreclosed mouth, report back
any stirrings still
not far from you.

Flooding big-
celled sleepyard.

Every partition overrun
by squadrons of gray.

The letters breaking out of line,
last
dreamproof tugs—each
with a vulture-claw
towing a part
of the still-
unsunken sign.

Go blind at once, today:
eternity too is full of eyes—
what helped the images
overcome their coming
drowns there;
there the fire goes out of
what spirited you away from language
with a gesture you let happen
like the waltz of two words
made of pure fall, silk, and nothing.

Ring narrowing Day under
the heavenleaf's web of veins.
Across large cells of empty time, through
rainfall, climbs
a black-blue thing: the
thought-beetle.

Words in blood-bloom
throng before his feelers.

At high noon, in
a humming of seconds,
to the round grave's shadow where I lie
already in my chambered pain
you come—for two days
of ochre and red
I spirited you off
to Rome with me
—sliding over thresholds, leveled, bright:

arms, only the arms that circle you
are visible. This much

of a mystery
I could muster still, in all's despite.

The hourglass buried
in peony-shadow:

when my thoughts finally come down
Pentecost Lane
they will inherit the Reich
where,
trapped in sand, you still
get whiffs of air.

Behind the charcoal surfaces of sleep—
our shanty is no secret—
our dream had swelled, cocky, fiery, in spite of everything,
and just as I drove gold nails into
that morning,
floating coffin-perfect down the stream

royally the rods shot down, divining
water—water came out!—
boats tore into macrosecond Memory,
slime-muzzled creatures drifted abroad—
no heaven yet had caught so many—
what a seine you were, really,
you so torn apart!—the creatures drifted, drifted,

horizons of salt
rose in our eyes, far out
in the abyss where a mountain was forming,
my world was calling yours
its own, forever.

Go back and add up
the shadows of all the steps
to that orchid—behind five hills of boyhood—
from there I'd win back
my half-word for twelve-night, from there
my hand would come to seize you
forever.

A little disaster helps, tiny as
the heartstop I
put after your eye
when it stammers my name.

You come too,
as if over pastures,
and bring along an image: gamblers
on the wharf.
Our housekeys were crossing each other
in a coat of arms, breaking the law;
meanwhile strangers were shooting craps
with what was left of
our language,
our lot.

Half-mauled, mask-
faced, a corbel-stone
deep
in the eyeslit-crypt:

inward, upward, toward
the cranial interior,
where you turn heaven over and over
in furrow and fold
he plants his image.
It outgrows itself, it grows out.

From fists white with the truth
of the beaten word-wall
a new brain breaks into bloom.

Beautiful, never ever to be veiled,
it casts the shadows
of its thought.
Twelve mountains, twelve brows,
shape up
in its steadfastness.

Even sadness,
your starry-eyed
gypsy, knows this place.

Noisemakers shoot into the light: it's the Truth
breaking the news.

Over there, the river-
bank is rising against us;
a black-lit
macro-mass—the
houses resurrected!—
raises its voice.

One ice thorn—even we
had cried out—
collects the clamor.

You forget you forget
the words turned flint in the fist,

flashes of punctuation
crystallize
at your wrist,

out of the earth's
cracked crests,
pauses come charging,

there, at
the sacrificial bush
where memory flares up,
you two are taken
in One breath.

Crackpots, decomposing
deeps.

If I were—

well, yes, if
I were that ash tree—bent
which way?—outside

I'd be able to
go along with you,
bright pan of gray, you and
the image growing through you
only at once to be
choked down,
and the two of you
caught
in the flashy, tight-drawn
noose of thought.

Lichtenberg's heir-
loom: twelve
nap-
kins and a tablecloth:
a celestial salute
to the ring
of fast
fading language
towers
inside the sign
zone.

All

—there's no heaven, no
earth, and the memory of both
is blotted out
down to one blue nut-
hatch trusting in the ash tree—

he had:
a white comet
picked up from the city ramparts.

A glottis, a voicecrack,
keeps it
in the uni-
verse.

Red: the loss
of thought-thread. The wailings
over it, the wailing
under it—whose voice is it?

In other words—don't ask
where—
I'd almost—
don't say where or when, again.

The sight of the songbirds at dusk,
through a ring of
ungraphed space,

made me promise myself weapons.

The sight of weapons, hands;
the sight of hands, the line
long since described by a flat, sharp
rock,

—you, wave,
carried it here, sharpened it,
you, Un-
losable One, gave yourself to it,
you, beach-sand, are the taker,
partaker,
you, shore-grass, drift
your share—

the line, the line
we swim through, twice each
millennium, tied up
in each other,
and not even the sea,
sublime unfathomable sea
that runs alive through us,
can believe
all the singing in our fingers.

Gurgling, then
vegetating quiet on the riverbanks.

One sluice left. At the
wartlike tower, glazed with
brine, you disgorge.

Ahead of you, where
giant sporangia paddle,
a luster sickles—
as if words were gagging there.

Frankfurt, September

Blind wall-space,
bearded by brilliances.
A dream of a cockchafer
sheds light on it.

Behind that, raster of lamentations,
Freud's forehead opens up:

the tear
compacted of silence
breaks out in a proposition:
"Psycho-
logy for the last
time."

The pseudo-jackdaw
(cough-caw's double)
is breakfasting.

The glottal stop is breaking
into song.

Coincidence staged, the signs all
unconsigned to wind, the number
multiplied, wrongs wreathed,
the Lord a closet-fugitive, rainfaller, eyeballer,
as lies turn blazing sevens, knives
turn flatterers, crutches
perjurors, U-
under
       this
             world,
the ninth one is already tunneling,
   O Lion,
sing the human song of
tooth and soul, the two
hard things.

Who
rules?

Our life—color-beleaguered, number-beset.

The clock
wastes time with the comet,
the knights
are anglers,
names
cover frauds with gold-leaf,
the hooded jewelweed
numbers the dots in the stone.

Pain as a snail's shadow.
I hear it's not getting later at all.
Here Bogus and Boring, back in the saddle,
set the pace.

Instead of you, there are halogen lamps.
Instead of our homes, light-traps,
terminus-temples.

Diaphanous, black,
the juggler's pennant
is at its
lowest point.

The hard-won Umlaut in the unword:
your light reflected: tunnel-shield
for a local
shade of thought.

Spasms, I love you, psalms,

O semensmeared one, feelwalls
deep in the gulch of you exult,

You, eternal, uneternitized,
eternitized, uneternal you,

selah,

into you, into you
I sing the scarscore of the bone-staff,

O red of reds, strummed far behind
the pubic hair, in caves,

out there, round and round
the infinite non of the canon,

you throw at me the nine-times-
twined
and dripping wreath
of trophy teeth.

Night in Pau

Henry IV rocking
in the royal tortoiseshell cradle:
immortality's number.
In its wake, it made
an eleatic mocking.

Later in Pau

In the corner of your eye,
stranger, the shadow of
the Albigenses—

after
the Waterlooplein market,
I'm singing of you
to the unmatched
canvas shoe, to the
Amen that gets hawked off with it,
in the lot
that's vacant for eternity; singing
you away:

so that Baruch, who never
cried,
may grind
around you his
precision-beveled
uncomprehended, all-seeing
tear.

The ounce of truth in the depths of delusion:

two pans of the scale
come by it,
in turns, both at
the same time, conversing.

Heaved to heart-height,
my son,
the law wins.

Lyon, Les Archers

Bristling in the brick
recess, the iron spike:
the neighboring millennium
with-
drawing into its otherness, unforthcoming,
follows
your wandering eyes.

Now,
the thrown dice of your glances
waken your neighbor,
she gets heavier
and heavier.

You, too, with all
your otherness,
with-
draw,
deeper and
deeper.

One
String
stretches its pain under you both.

Oh bow, the missing target
looms.

Sleep-pieces, wedges
driven into nowhere:
we remain constant,
steered round,
the star
concurs.

Attached to out-cast
dream relics, Truth
comes down, a child,
over the ridge.

In the valley,
buzzed-about by
clods of earth,
by spray of scree,
by seeds of eye,
the crutch
leafs through the
No that blooms
crown-high.

Graygreens
from nearby water-shafts
dug out by unawakened hands:

the depths
yield up their growth
without resistance,
without a sound.

Save it,
before
the Stone Day has blown dry
the swarms of men
and beasts, just
as the seven-reed flute mandates,
in front of mouth and muzzle.

Chitin sunlings,
newly hatched.

Armored amphibians
wrap themselves up
in blue prayer-shawls, the sand-
dependent gull calls out in the
affirmative, the furtive
fire-leaf
thinks things over.

Eternities dead
and gone,
a letter touches
your still-un-
injured fingers,
a shining countenance
comes somersaulting in
and touches down in
smells, sounds.

Hothouse of an asylum
emptied out by
prayers;
pretty little saxifrage
growing in the
grouting;

a glazed look
dozes through
the half-opened
door;

an over-
aged syllable comes
gangling in—

woken up,
the blind man's cane
points out its place
behind the manes of the white horses.

Lucky, the
mummy-leap over the
mountain.

Lonely, the giant
paulownia leaf
that makes a note.

Big toy worlds are
left lying about. Stars
entirely idle.

In their control towers
one hundred silver hooves
hammer free the outlawed light.

On the rainsoaked rutted road, silence,
the gleeman, delivering his little sermon.

As if you could hear.
As if I still loved you.

White noises, bundled
light-
lines
over the table
with its message-in-a-bottle.

(Listening in, listening in to
an ocean, drinking it in, in
addition; removing the veil
over road-weary
mouths.)

One secret
gets mixed into the word forever.
(Whosoever falls therefrom
rolls beneath a leafless tree.)

Audible-inaudible:
all the
shadow-stoppers
logging on
at all the
shadow-links.

Your heart manholed
for the installation of feeling.

Your great motherland made
of prefab parts.

Your milk-sister
a shovel.

Here are the industrious
mineral resources (domestic)

here the heated-up syncope

here the insoluble riddle
of the jubilee year

here the glassed-in
spider altars in the facility's
overarching sprawl

here the half-sounds
(still there?),
shades' palaver

here the ice-adjusted fears
cleared for flight

here the semantically X-rayed
sound-proof shower-room,
with its baroque appointments

here the unscrawled wall
of a cell:

live your life right
through here, without a clock.

When I don't know, when I don't know,
without you, without you, without a You,

they all come,
acephalic by choice,
the brainless life-laureates
of the Youless
people of the lord:

Ashrei,

a word with no meaning,
transtibetan,
ejaculated into
the helmeted ovaries
of Pallas
Athena
the Jewess,

and when he,

he,

foetal,

strums a Carpathian not-not,

then the
Allemande
starts tatting
her im-
mortal self-sick
song.

Gigantic,
trackless, tree-
studded
hand-
tract,

Quincunx.

The branches, guided by nerves,
swoop down on
the already
red-tipped deep shadow,
a snakebite before
Rose-
rise.

Day freed from demons.
All breeze.

Disenchanted, the powers-that-be
sew up the stabbed lung.
Blood pours back in.

In Böcklemünd cemetery, the
hammershine from
infinity
races over the
shallow inscription on the front,
also over you,
deep Brother Letter.

Husks of the finite, stretchable—
and inside each
another shape takes root.

One thousand isn't yet
once one.

Each arrow you shoot off
carries its own target
into the decidedly
secret
tangle.

Wet from the world
the scrapped taboos—
and all the bordercrossings between them,
pursuing
meaning, fleeing
meaning.

Hush, you hag, and ferry me across the rapids.
Eyeflash, aim ahead.

Eyeshot's island, broken
into heartscript
in the quick of night, faintly lit
by an ignition key.

Even this seemingly
starstudded altitude
is overcrowded
with destination-driven forces.

The wide-open stretch we longed for
hits us head-on.

Eternity gets older: at
Cerveteri the asphodels
worry one another white
with questions.

Their ladles murmuring
over stone, over stone,
they spoon out soup
in all the beds
in all the camps
from dead men's dishes.

It's late. A spongy fetish
eats the cones off the Christmas tree;

a wish frisks after them
roughened up by
aphorisms of frost;

the window flies open; we're outside;

the bump of Being
will not level out;

a nose-heavy
stunt-happy cloud
carries us above it
and away.

Come, we are cutting out
nerve cells
from the
rhomboid
fossae
—multipolar duckweed,
ponds spotlit till blank—

From still-reachable centers
ten fibers drag
half-recognizable things.

Free of dross, free of dross.

If we were blades now,
drawn as of old
in the pergola in Paris, one eyeglow long,

the arctic bull
would come bounding down
and crown its horns with us

and gore and gore.

Soul-blind behind the ashes,
in the sacro-senseless word,
the rhyme-stripped one comes striding,
brain-mantle draped over his shoulders,

auditory canal ringing
with networked vowels,
he decomposes the visual purple,
he composes it.

Next-door-neighbor Night.
Dwarf or giant-sized—it all
depends on the cut in the fingerpad,
on what
comes out of it.

At times super-eyed
when biconcave
a thought, out of elsewhere,
comes dripping in.

The ropes, stiff with salt water:
this time
the white
mainstay can't be untied.

Nearby, on the sandbar's eelgrass,
in the anchor's shadow,
a name makes fun of the
untwinned
riddle.

Out of angel flesh, on
Insufflation Day, in
phallic union with the One
—He the enlivener, He the just, made you sleep to me,
sister—,
we stream up through the channels, up
into the crown of roots:
parted,
it lifts us high, makes us co-eternal,
brain at hand, a bolt of lightning
sews up our skulls, the pans
and all
the bones not yet disseminated:

seed scattered in the East to be gathered in the West, co-eternal—,

where this writing burns, after
three-quarters death, before
the tossing and turning scrap
of a soul that
quakes with crown-fear
ever since ever began.

Upholster the word-hollows
with panther pelt,

enlarge them, furback and furforth,
senseback and senseforth,

give them vestibules, ventricles, valves,
furnish them with wilds, parietal,

and listen for the second,
every time their second, second
sound.

Walls of speech, space inwards—
wound into yourself,
you rave your way to the very last one.

The fogs burn off.

The heat sinks in.

Four ells of earth
orphaned in the storm-trough,

The heavenly logbook
blotched with ash,

Michael muck-mouthed,
Gabriel mire-gagged,

dough soured, in a stone flash.

Naked under death leaves,
their bodies both unsullied,
both defaced.

Pulled up on shore
by the whitest root of
the whitest tree.

Stone of incest, rolled away.

An eye cut out
from the doctor's kidney
stands in for Hippocrates
at the cosmetic perjury.

Salvos, sleep-bombs, gold gas.

I'm floating, I'm floating

As loud colors, heaped up
in the evening, species of being
come back:
a quarter-monsoon
without a place to rest,
a hail of prayer
before inflamed
eyelidlessness.

The chimney-swallow, sister
to the arrow, stood at the zenith.

The One of the air-clock
flew at the hour-hand,
deep into its chime.

The shark
spat out the live Inca.

It was land-grab time
in the state of Humanity.

Everything went around
like us, with seals broken.

White, white, white
like paint on pickets
the laws line up
and march
right in.

Haut Mal

O irredeemable
beloved, sleep-attacked,
tainted by the gods:

your tongue is sooty,
your urine black,
your stool a bilious liquefaction,

like myself,
you use
foul language;

you put one foot before the other,
lay one hand atop the other,
burrow into goatskin,

consecrate
my cock.

The golfball growth
in the neck:
God's arithmetical
brain-teaser
for the full-head
hairpiece,

a place
to test the one-
of-a-kind chest
pain, revealing
the future, blithe
as a fiber of steel.

Windfield bound for winter: this
is where you must live, granular, like a pomegranate
concealing
the crust of early frost,
with a darkening penstroke
across the goldyellow shadow of
your star-spattered wing—
     yet you were never
     only bird or fruit—
the supersonic wing
you
songed into being.

Who stood that round?

The weather was clear. We were drinking

aboard the great Wreck of the Solstice,
and singing the Shanty of Ash.

Audio-visual vestiges in
sleep ward 1001.

Night and day,
the Bear Polka:

they're re-educating you:

you'll be
a him
again.

Knock out
the chocks of light:

adrift, the word
belongs to dusk.

Eternities swept
over his face and
onward.

A blaze slowly extinguished
every wick and candle.

A green, out of this world,
covered with down the chin of
the stone, the one the orphans
kept burying and re-
burying.

She of the freckled farewells
is reading your palm
faster than
fast.

The blue of her Irish eyes is growing through her,
win and loss
at once:

distance,
O you
hand of glances.

Degenerate
goddess:

spindly-limbed,
friend of grief,

between your genuflecting legs
a knowing knife
turns on
its axis,
contravening
the blood.

Assembly-
line facility:

razzle-dazzle in the half-dark,

—the healing hand lay
on you, remember, under the fit-
ful flares—

the protective word
in a pressurized helmet,
a punctuation mark
for fresh-air vent.

Soul-welding, arc-light.

In their cases,
the lovely rhymy metal bellows
are being given
artificial respiration.

Weather hand—
the bog puddle shows it the way
through the dark paludal wood.

Luminescence.

One who, one-
legged, pedals the peat organ bellows
gets for his efforts a bright shaft
of loss.

Nightsources, distant
destination-points
on god watch,

your slopes in the Thou
of the heart, O Brainmount,
are brimming with foam.

We always find ourselves
here,
my earth-mate:

unwashed, unpainted,
in the shafthead
of the beyond where

a
conveyor
running late
passes through us, through the cloud scatter,
up and down, up and down—

inside is insurgent
whistling, mischief
afoot—

against the iridescent orb
the flight shadow
scars us over at level
seven—

close to ice age
two swans of felt
steer around the floating
stone-icon

Lilac twilight daubed with yellow windows,

Jacob's star-staff over
Rubble Terminal,

time to play with matches, so far
no intercurrencies,

from a nice bar
to an ice bar.

You with the dark slingshot,
you with the stone:

It's a night from today.
I cast a light behind myself.
Bring me down, get
serious with us.

I gave a chance
to your, even to your,
false-rung shade,

I lapidated it with my
true-shaded, true-
rung self—a
six-point star.

Today,
take quiet where you wish.

Trashing time's
dishonored things, taking
no heart, I, even I, am already
going home, out into the street,
into the stony many.

Proverb on the Wall

Defaced (a renovated angel ceases to be)
a head comes into its own,

sharpsighted,
the astral
weapon
with its stock of memory
salutes
the
lions of its thought.

The aural apparatus drives a flower.
You are its year,
the world with no tongue
persuades you,
every sixth one
knows that.

Open glottis, air flow,
the
vowel, active
with its one
formant,

consonant concussions, the
evidence largely screened out,

shield against stimuli: consciousness,

unoccupiable
I and you, too,

superveri-
fied
the eye-greedy
memory-greedy
rolling
brand-
name,

the temporal lobe intact,
likewise the optic stem.

Raised bog, in the shape of
a watch-crystal (someone has time).

So many swallowtails, sick on sundew.

Out of the
drainage ditch
a menorah of mullein stands up.

Quaking bog, if you turn into turf
I'll unhand the clockwork of
the Just.

Particles, patriarchs, buried
in the upheaval, spangles
of ore.

You make the most of things
with them,
as if angiosperms
were having a
forthright
word
with you.

Shofar traced in limestone.

In karst caverns
what is lost gains
rarity, clarity.

And force and pain
and what pushed
and drove and held me:

jubilee leap-
years,

rush of pine scent (once upon a time),

the unlicensed conviction
there ought to be another way
of saying
this.

A reading branch, just one,
feeding your forehead,

a source of light you
drowsily swallow
passes through the hungry
host-tissue,

seeing-aid, layer-streaked,
over the moon-touched
backscatter probes. Macroscale: microscale.

Still, there are earths, earths.
Cornea-coated basalt,
kissed by spacecraft:
cosmic
orbital-show, and yet:
landlocked horizons.

Terrestrial, terrestrial.

A reading branch, just one,
feeding the forehead—as if you were writing
poems—,
it lands on the picture-postcard—
that was before
the bloodclot, on the threshhold
of the lungs—a year away, greetings from Pilsen,
a year around,
time-wild from so much
quiet unfurling:

Bon vent, bonne mer,

a flapping
occipital lobe, a
glimpse of the sea,
is hoisting, right where you live,
its un-
conquerable
capital.

The cables have already been laid
to happiness past
and its logistical
lines,

and ahead
in the cantonment areas
where they're spraying wellness agents,
mild melodic antidotes
signal
the final sprint
through your conscience.

The splintering echo, darkened,
heading for
the brainstream,

hesitating
at the bend's levee,

massive
absence of windows
over there,
take a look,

that pile
of idle supplications,
one
buttstock blow away
from the prayer-silos,

one and none.

Nowhere, with its silken veil,
dedicates its dureé to daytime,

here I can see
you.

Visitors can come and go, where you are—

sleeping unmonitored
under its sand-cap,
your brain
steers its way
through the one
unforfeitable
oceanic
day,

come, I'm brightening up,

come, my inbred one,
my heavy one,
I'm giving you
to me, and you to you, too.

In the most remote of
secondary senses, at the foot
of the paralyzed stairway of amens:
Existence, a phase
stripped bare.

Nearby, in the gutter,
common wisdoms
still wriggling.

Sleep secreted the contour,
dream fiber strengthened it.
At its single
heart-beaten temple
ice is forming.

No book opens up.

The Supernothing threw
its lot with me;
all ice,
it gives up the fight.

We're ready
to trade away our mortal inmost.

No reply—the thorn
climbs up through the cradles.

Behind the time clock,
time, immune to fools,
is giving itself away.

O little root of a dream
you hold me here
undermined by blood,
no longer visible to anyone,
property of death.

Curve a face
that there may be speech, of earth,
of ardor, of
things with eyes, even
here, where you read me blind,

even
here,
where you
refute me,
to the letter.

Don't sign your name
between worlds,

surmount
the manifold of meanings,

trust the tearstain,
learn to live.

Page 1: Voices, scored into

Celan worked on this untitled sequence of lyrics between 1956 and 1958. A polyphonic composition for seven voices and none (the coda's "No voice"), it inaugurates his 1959 collection *Sprachgitter*, which ends with another major polyphonic composition, "Engführung" (known in English as "Stretto" and "Straitening"). Celan mimics the interweaving of voices in music by means of sonic and semantic recall and anticipation. For example, in the third lyric, the voices are bell "ropes" and in the next lyric this word begets the image of a gallows; heart (*Herz*), invoked first in connection with the mother, then parenthesized as *part* of an adjective in the sixth lyric, recalls the "carpel" bleeding sap (*Harz*), in the coda; the typographical parentheses reappear as "brackets"—and so on. Aimed at what is familiar and secure in the German language (from compound words and common phrases to traditional poetic tropes), such a poetic procedure begins with analysis of the word and ends in ontological resynthesis of the world.

In his 1960 speech "The Meridian," Celan discusses art as the place where one can "set onself free as an—estranged—I" and gives the example of Georg Büchner's character Lenz who is "bothered that he could not walk on his head." A man who walks on his head, Celan says, "sees the sky below, as an abyss." Poetic existence partakes of the groundless and the grotesque. The shell of death in the third lyric recalls an ancient Jewish burial device, a seashell carved within a fret. Jacob's brother is Esau. Martin Buber relates the words of Schmelke von Nikolsburg to the effect that the Messiah won't come before Esau's tears have ceased to flow: "The children of Israel [. . .] shall they weep in vain, as long as the children of Esau shed tears? But 'the tears of Esau'—that does not mean the tears which the peoples weep and you do not weep; they are the tears which all human beings weep when they ask something" (*Tales of the Hasidim*).

Page 5: With wine and being lost, with

Many of Celan's later poetological studies are informed by the tension between voice (the traditional medium of the lyric) and inscription. Voice, by definition, is single and always already articulated in a specific tongue; a grapheme, on the other hand, can be shared by several writing conventions. Celan's own linguistic predicament gives this commonplace a twist: All the languages he used were, in some sense, foreign (Lacoue-Labarthe); none could provide the security of an indubitably voiced lyric subjectivity. Hence, many poems contain what one might call *translingual effects*. For example, in the poem at hand, *Neige* means "remainder," "end," "dregs" in German; the "same" grapheme in French spells the word "snow." The phrase is hardly over when snow literally befalls the poem in line 3. To the English eye, *neige* also moves in the nearness of "neigh" (God's "song"!) and its homonym "nay." The latter, retranslated into a German verb (*negieren*), brings us back, with a difference, almost to the place where the translingual steeple-chase started.

A corresponding tension obtains between presentation and representation. The representers, that is, those who busily and fearfully make sense out of the sheer music of sound (animal? divine?), are exposed as liars. One of the poem's drafts suggests the proximity, for Celan, of things understandable (*verständlich*) and things imaged or illustrated (*bebildert*). Against the attempt to contain the music in understandable transcription or visual images, the poem broadcasts its iconoclastic resistance to reason and pours Nietzschean scorn on the attempt to trap art—or divinity—in images. Translators, among others, thus encounter a troubling image of their enterprise; hence our commitment, here and elsewhere, as much to a translatorial reconstruction of meaning as to the phono-graphic fundamentals of Celan's poems.

German *Wein*, wine, is paronymically very near to *weinen*, cry, weep; with regard to the poem's poetology it's worthwhile to remember Joel 1.5: "Awake, ye drunkards and weep; and howl, all ye drinkers of wine, because of the new wine; for it is cut off from your mouth." It's also noteworthy that Celan's poem quotes from (alludes to) the translation that institutes modern German, Luther's Bible; namely, from Jeremiah 25. And here translation runs into an aporia: to translate a translation is not to translate precisely the fact that it is a translation.

Page 6: THREESOME, FOURSOME

The poem is a variation on a Romanian folksong pattern. Our translation foregrounds the self-reflexive language of the original. The poem is also a part of Celan's poetic dialogue with Nelly Sachs, in *Die Niemandsrose*.

Page 7: ERRATIC

An "erratic" boulder is one transported from its original place by a glacier (geol.). In the sensibility of an exile battered and displaced by history's drifts, this scientific definition resounds with personal pain. More generally, "stone" functions as a nodal grapheme and metaphor in Celan's work. Celan's "language of the stone" (James Lyon's term) encompasses language drawn from the sciences of the physical world: geology, mineralogy, crystallography, glaciation, fossilization, etc., and probes sedimentations and enstonements in language and myth, memory and the psyche. Indeed, Celan sees the very tradition of European lyricism in terms of stone: from Petrarca (whose name comes from "stone") to Mandelstam (whose first book was entitled *Stone* and who inspired some of Celan's most interesting work as a translator). Celan's neologistic metaphor *Kriechstern* sees the movement of a star, across a sky that is at once crepuscular and languaged, in terms of slow glacial movement (geol. creep = slow movement of rock debris down a weathered slope). Celan's notes for "The Meridian" shed further light on the poetological significance of this poem: today's poem seeks its initial voice in *muta cum liquida*, the combination of voiceless and liquid consonant.

Page 9: To one who stood outside the door, one

Inspired by the Golem legend, this enigmatic poem of creation and transgression, language and ashes, echoes a variety of sources (including Kafka's parable "Before the Law"). Whatever its origins, the poem leads to the center of Celan's intense reflection on the other at the self's door (no less outside than already inside); on the essence of art and language, and their fateful alignments with death; on the human, the quasi-human, and the legion of ambiguous apparatuses, automatons, and technologies straddling the life-death line.

In his "The Meridian," Celan cites Lenz's reflections on art ("One would like to be the Medusa's head" to seize the natural as the natural by means of art), and comments: "Here we have stepped beyond human nature, gone outwards, and entered a mysterious realm, yet one turned towards that which is human, the same realm where the monkey, the robots and, accordingly . . . alas, art, too, seem to be at home." (tr. Jerry Glenn)

The great Rabbi Loew of Prague (c. 1520–1609), apostrophized by the speaker, is a legendary figure credited with the creation of the Golem (lit. a "formless mass"), a clay humanoid endowed with life but separated from death by next-to-nothing, a mere mark. As Gerschom Scholem glosses the legend in his study of the Kaballa and its symbolism, the Golem lives by the inscription on his forehead of the Hebrew word '*emeth* (truth); bereft of the aleph at the head of the word, the Golem collapses into a pile of ashes (Heb. *meth* = (he is) dead). The Hebrew word for "nothing(ness)," K. Reichert points out, likewise begins with the mute aleph. The imperative to circumcise the word for the nameless and perhaps unnameable One-outside-the-door (provided that all "one's" in the poem refer to one one) involves the extremes, on the one hand, of ritual acceptance and life and, on the other, of rejection and death.

Pages 11: Flung wood

A "boomerang" shot "from Nothingness" into the bull's-eye of a soul appears in Celan's earlier poem "But." Lat. *lapillus* = little stone, esp. voting pebble (white for acquittal, black for condemnation). With this allusion, Celan's boomerang of a poem "returns" to the first European poet of exile, Ovid. In Metamorphoses XV, Myscelus is commanded by Hercules to leave his own country, and the god's command (accompanied by dreadful threats lest he disobey) puts him in a mortal double bind, for the penalty for defection is death. Myscelus is brought to trial; each pebble dropped in the urn is black, but when the pebbles are poured for the count they are all white (Hercules has interfered), and Myscelus is free. Celan's interest in this allegory of exile and death is understandable. Unlike the speculative return of spirit to itself, Celan's projectile returns utterly othered and bereft of origins (un-referenced, as a latent pun in the original, heard by Hamacher, suggests). There is no kill, no gain; indeed, apart from a pure indication of time, it is impossible to tell what, if anything, returns.

In a poem of literally attenuated and broken German (Celan's line-breaks often tear words asunder as if to emphasize that the site of pain, the jointure that divides, is inside words), the rhyme rhyme–home (*Reim–heim*) at the poem's turning point seems to mark the ruin of a poetics of homecoming. (As noted by Jerry Glenn, this is no casual rhyme for Celan: It holds together the final distich of his early poem "The Graves' Nearness," in which the speaker asks his (dead) mother if she can still bear, as she once did, at home, the painful soft German rhyme.)

Page 12: How low could it go, my once immortal word

"Bad language" (profanity, blasphemy, obscenity) frequently intrudes into the elegiac lyricism of Celan's later poetry. Celan's focus on language as a whole, synchronically as well as diachronically, leads him to a scandal that involves the fundamental philosophemes and theologoumena of the European tradition. It would suffice, at this point, just to remember the fervor invested in Hegel's early theological and other writings; for instance, "How could they [the Jews] have an inkling of beauty who saw in everything only matter?" And, even more to the point: "The Jewish multitude was bound to wreck his [Jesus'] attempt to give them the consciousness of something divine, for faith in something divine, something great, cannot make its home in a dunghill. The lion has no room in a nest, the infinite spirit none in the dungeon of a Jewish soul, the whole of life none in a withering leaf &&&." It would be idle to argue whether Celan's poem really "quotes" Hegel's word *Kot* (dreck), even though the incarnational metaphor that frames the whole poem suggests more than a mere coincidence. This is Celan's poetological anguish: His poetic utterance or breath is in advance immersed in the language of the aesthetic tradition Hegel speaks out of and for; can a total release from it be purchased only as total silence?

But the question of voice (logos) and its (shit)house cannot be resolved by a simple condemnation of Hegel's language as a historical manifestation of (philosophical, Christian) anti-Semitism. Over and beyond his own personal bias, Hegel could be said to give voice to a fundamental, onto-theological, anxiety which is older than the Christian topic of the incarnation and which makes anti-Semitism historically possible: the anxiety, to cite another text of Hegel's, that "every animal finds a voice in its violent death; it expresses itself as eliminated/superseded [*aufgehobnes*] self)." The animal voice is thus, always already, the voice of death (Giorgio Agamben): the resounding sound Herder heard at the origin of language. Voice pays this mad toll to the infinite for its sojourn in matter.

The starflower (*trientalis europea*), native to the eastern Carpathians, has seven points, hence its German name, seven-pointed star. Flower, star, and poetic word constitute a central imagistic trinity, in Celan's work. In the present context, seven and star also recall the Pleiades. If the inversion of the "natural" vertical turns heaven into an abyss (see note to "Voices"), here the abyss is further interiorized in a Rilkean conflation of cosmos and inner space, with the crucial difference that the Celanian interior is a vile–brainy–body. Celan's ambivalence regarding the "immortal" poetic word is a fallout from the poem immediately preceding the present poem in *Die Niemandsrose*: In it, the poetic "you" observes "us" from the chalice of a Ghetto-Rose, "immortal from so many deaths died on morning paths."

Page 13: PAIN, THE SYLLABLE

This poem not only engages in dialogue Rilke's majestic Tenth Elegy but re-cants and re-spells the entire tradition of visionary poetry in the West, its premises and means, its meanings, and the meaningless. (The initial letters of the nouns in the original title spell an ominous SS.)

The poem declares its ontological search with its very first words. German *Es gab* ("it gave") is also the idiom for the gift of being, a dative dynamic missing from the English "there was."

The flower of Columbus's quest is the *Colchicum autumnale* (erroneously known, in English, as the autumn crocus), a flower with an emblematic presence in Celan, on account of its poetic genealogy and suggestive Latin and German names. Colchinium comes from Colchis, the mythical land of the Golden Fleece, and was associated with the black arts of its princess, Medea (it contains a poisonous alkaloid); later, the troubadours associated it with the menace of the Lady's eyes; in modern times, Apollinaire, whose poetry Celan cherished and translated, revived the legend in "Les Colchiques." The German name of the *colchinium* means, literally, "timeless" (hence its importance in a poem that explores history's beginnings and ends); it is also known as the "Naked Whore" and "Naked Virgin" (both latent in connection with Columbus). As an ambiguous emblem of the entire European poetic tradition, the colchinium reflects Celan's own ambivalence vis-à-vis what he inherits and is outcast from. Just a few lines later Celan explores—indeed, deflowers, reflowers—the anagogic Rosa Mundi. To capture some of the resonances in Celan's poem, we used another (unfortunately, innocent) flower, the immortelle, hoping that the markers of time, death, and privation/loss (*todlos–Zeitlose*; deathless—immortelle) will thicken the translation's texture in a manner suggestive of the original's richness.

At midpoint Celan constructs a complex spatio-temporal figure, conflating rose season (fall) and time of day (nightfall). Furthermore, taking advantage of the term "wind-rose" (the face of the compass), Celan projects an image of complete loss of orientation: The wind-rose has lost its points/petals, become black/blank, so the instrument of orientation is unruly and useless. And yet the burst of nightbloom is a luminous dawn. Black light is, after all, a light, a contralight (backlight)—the light of letters? As the poem's further progress indicates, this nautico-stellar wordscape recalls Mallarmé's Master, the Septentrion above his shipwrecked head, but Celan doesn't seem content with the ironic consolations of constellar art.

The precious stones that follow the imagery of new day refract a variety of Judeo-Christian visionary texts and ancient rituals (Egyptian burial practices); for example, in Revelations 21, the New Jerusalem has twelve foundations of precious stone, each kind of stone corresponding to one of the twelve tribes. But for Celan the Apocalypse (Auschwitz, the end of time) has already occurred; the annihilation that makes his poetry possible also makes meaning well impossible—casts a shadow on any attempt to articulate a new world vision.

The last lines of the original perform a characteristic Celanian stutter, spelling—and stumbling at—the incommensurability between pain and articulable language. Pain (a word conspicuously absent from the body of the poem) gnaws away at the ends and means of poetic inscription—even as it constitutes (spells) the poem's condition of (im)possibility. In German this stutter (*buch-, buch-, buch- / stabierte, stabierte*) follows the bimorphemic structure of the verb *buchstabieren* (from *Buch-stab*, "letter"), which means "to spell." The ending also recalls Mallarmé's puns *"l'alphabet des astres"* (in "*Quant au livre*"), the "alphabet of stars," which sounds like "*alphabet disastre*," and "*sur les cendres des astres*" (in "Igitur"). The density of self-reference and language involution in the poem's finale suggested a number of parographic possibilities (e.g., a litter of little alphabeasts in the alphabyss), but the question was to find a rendition in tune with Celan's pain-ful economy.

Page 15: LA CONTRESCARPE

Taking its title from Place de la Contrescarpe, Paris (Celan's ultimate station of exile), the poem recalls the public and private calendars of the poet's life story. As the foreign title indicates, it is "about" the experience of being translated and dwelling in translation, a narrative struggling to make meaningful a foreign name, place of exile. (Cp. Merrill's "Lost in Translation.")

Celan's first trip to France (to study medicine) took place in 1938; by a fateful coincidence, his train stopped at Anhalter Station, Berlin, on the morning after Kristallnacht (November 9/10, 1938), which saw Nazi-led pogroms of Jewish synagogues, businesses, schools, and homes throughout Germany. Nine years later—a Holocaust later, a hiatus of time history cannot recuperate but must not be allowed to forget—in 1948, Celan will arrive at Place de la Contrescarpe again. The poem seems to center on a Fourteenth of July (1948), from which it counts back nine years (nine other July 14th's), to Celan's first journey to France, and forward through fourteen years of exile in Paris. This series of private and painful July 14th's may be Celan's grimly ironic comment on the emancipatory hopes aroused by the French Revolution (the series of its public anniversaries, after all, leads through many horrors all the way to the Russian Revolution and then the Holocaust); or an equally grim reminder that today's mindlessly festive crowd may turn, tomorrow, to orgies of hatred and destruction; and that historical crimes are all-too-easily forgotten or distanced. The Celanian poem doesn't know the shelter of distance, historical or aesthetic. A crystal of memory and breath, it always dwells on the verge of Kristallnacht. The past is always imminent.

While the details of Celan's life story have been ably reconstructed (see John Felstiner's *Paul Celan: Poet, Survivor, Jew*), some of the language of the poem remains open to conjecture in a way that precludes even a remotely literal rendition. Two recent state-of-the-art volumes, *Paul Celan, Die Niemandsrose: Vorstufen, Textgenese, Endfassung* (Suhrkamp 1996) and *Kommentar zu Paul Celans "Die Niemandsrose"* / hrsg. von Jürgen Lehmann (Heidelberg, 1997), address those conjecturable moments. As can be expected from a work concerned with autobiographical reflection, the poem alludes to other poems included in *Die Niemandsrose*, to Celan's early work, and to the work of Hölderlin, among others.

"All the clouding around her": The cloud formation (*Gewölk*) can be read as a condensation of cloud and people (*Volk*), the Jewish people gone up in smoke. We count on English readers to hear a hint of "crowding" around our gerund. Cp. Celan's own compound "*das Volk-vom-Gewölk*" (the "people of clouds"), which occurs in the poem "*Hüttenfenster*" (separated from "La Contrescarpe" only by "Pain, the Syllable"). Cp. also "Radix, Matrix" in Hamburger.

Paulownia tomentosa (or princess tree) is an oriental tree with paired heart-shaped leaves. Celan's botanical knowledge is always contextually relevant: The poem opens with a tree. The fact that the poet shares his first name with the tree (*Paulownia*) should not go unnoticed.

"Cross Cut, Copy Cat, and Ugly Mug" is an attempt to match Celan's inventive compounding of violence, aesthetic fraud and bestiality. The "second coming" hinted at in the poem's last lines has, not the Yeatsian dimension of horror ("what rough beast"), but rather an Arendtian disappointment at banality: The Lord has a banner (like a politician) and a camera (like a tourist). So too the Bible's dove, which flew from the ark to find safety, here was never able to come back with its branch of sign, and soon is lapped or dovetailed into a keel of its own. But despite the sorry prospects, the eye of the instrument itself (the lens of the camera, the watch-face of time, and the mind's own eye, which the observant poet trains both inward and outward) cannot turn away: and it is trained on the transparent, in order to sort semblance from resemblance, value from value, crystal from crystal, breath from air.

Page 17: Floated down blackwater rapids

The feminine figure in the second stanza arises literally out of the poem's grammar, German being a gender-inflected language. Here and in other similar cases, a zero-gender Engish noun won't do since that would lead to an identification, along gender lines, between the figure addressed and the speaker. Without going into the vexed and ultimately misleading question as to who Celan's "you" might be—Celan's murdered mother, in some poems; Celan's wife, in others; an alter ego of the speaker, and so on—it suffices to say here that the "you" is grammatically (and sometimes semantically) gendered as feminine. (We've added similar cue-words in other poems to indicate imperative moods that otherwise might be taken for effects of Celan's characteristic comma-splicing.) The possibility that the you's referent is not a human figure but an allegorized abstract noun opens up intriguing interpretive paths (e.g., time and language are feminine nouns in German, and this poem can be read, metapoetically, as a poem "about" language and time), but translated into English this possibility results in the pathetic fallacy. Therefore, we resorted to an explicitly feminine human figure, well aware that making explicit the implicit (e.g., the grammatical) *limits* the readings.

Page 18: Gray-white of sheer

The sensory organs without their heads are figures of detachment that recall a gallery of such organs including Van Gogh's ear and Buñuel's sliced eye. Coming after such mixed sensory materials as gray-white feeling and sand blown over smoke, these severed attentions seem all the more (literally, etymologically) critical.

Page 19: (I know you: you're the one who's bent so low

The parentheses enclosing this poem suggest that it is an aside of sorts, relative to the *Atemwende* poems immediately adjacent to it. Despite the fact that our selection does not contain those two poems, we decided to retain the parentheses whose muteness on the massively white Celanian page is so eloquent.

Page 20: Singable remainder—trace

Among Celan's jottings for the poem is the following: "Readable outline—split, / bloodless lip." But he went further, seeking a trope that, rather than fix the sense exclusively, would allow of sense-in-progress, from physical freezing and dismemberment to legal incapacitation (barring the speaker from dialogue), so in his final version the lip became *entmündigte*, from the legal term *entmündigen*, to certify as incapacitated or rule as unable to testify; to put in guardianship); read down into its morphemes, *entmündigte* also suggests something of special "poetic" interest: bereft-of-mouth (for the poet's mouth logos and phusis are the same). We settled on "fore-closed" as suggesting in a single word an effect at once juridical and anatomical.

Page 21: Flooding, big

Verbally as well as in some particulars of spatial organzation, the location of this poem (*Schlafbau*) recalls Kafka's story "*Der Bau*." Just as in Kafka the subterranean quarters become indistinguishable from the builder's mind and narrative, in Celan's poem events appear at once external and internal (inside a consciousness on the verge of sleep), as well as intro-verbal. In other words, what occurs on the level of the letter jells and dissolves our perception of both inside and outside. In any case, the ambiguous events of this poem reflect Celan's constant search not for a language of transcendence but for a transcendence of language—at least, of language as arbitrary signification, premised upon decidabilities of container and content. Celan's suspension of instrumental language is a step beyond so-called self-reflexive poetry: The sign (already conceived here as graphic rather than phonic substance) is about to be scuttled and submerged under the reflective (narcissistic) surface, with no hope for speculative return. All the poem's events are in-vented.

The term *Bau* (construction, structure, etc.) has a wide range of meanings; Kafka's story is known in English as "The Burrow." We chose to render Celan's rich, polyvalent neologism as "sleepyard," in keeping with the cluster of boatyard images and nautical associations. The bird-barge-letter formation comes from Homer, possibly mediated by Mandelstam's poem "Insomnia." (Hermes invented the letters of the Greek alphabet in imitation of the wedge-shaped formation of cranes in flight.)

Page 23: Ring narrowing Day under

Celan opens this poem with a flourish, coining a tripartite compound, *Engholztag*. His neologism has the structure of a word for a calendar-day; moreover, the day in question is a day of "narrow annulus"; that is, the coinage combines two of Celan's nodal terms, the ring and narrowness, into a figure of stunted growth and destitution. In arboreal time, of course, a narrow annulus is the sign of a dry *year*. The violent and beautiful logic of the metaphor thus collapses two units of time, day (the punctual, the special moment) and year (the cyclical, the repetitive). And this metaphoric collapse of scale leads to further compacting of vastly different magnitudes as attention swoops from the celestial to the cellular. The poem bases its economy and music on the effects of passage through a place of constriction (or *Engführung*, as the eponymous poem from *Sprachgitter* has it). "Expand art?" asks Celan in "The Meridian." "No: rather go with art into your ownmost narrowness. And set yourself free."

The ending of the poem is ambiguous: The constriction effect has blurred the difference between blood and blossom, and it is suggestively unclear whether (human?) words are endowed with animality (blood), are smeared with blood, or are not themselves bloodthirsty carnivorous flowers (which elsewhere captivated Celan's attention: see "Raised bog").

Page 25: At high noon, in

Another study in ring structures. The poem's time, midday, literally translates Celan's nodal notion, the *meridian*, while the "round graves" it alludes to are in the Etruscan necropolis at Cerveteri, near Rome. A ring within a ring, the memory of a vanished race leads to the lovers' embrace, the encounter of self and (vanished) other, self as other, the meeting of the circle—all "protagonists" are in a sense sheer figures of time, that is, hours—always the same (cyclically) and different (chronologically).

Page 25: The hourglass buried

The last line of this poignant miniature ("*wo du versandend verhoffst*") presents a major problem, in that it epitomizes an essential aspect of the Celanian poetics. *Verhoffen*, etymologically derived from "hope" and contradictorily glossed as "to hope fervently" or "to give up hope"(!), is a venery term: an animal (e.g., deer) *verhoff*'s when it pauses, stockstill, alert, sensing the wind for danger, etc. The verb thus names a figure of time suspended or arrested; here it is a figure inside the time piece. This characteristic Celanian turn makes it impossible to think of the poem in terms of the "still moment" or stasis of beauty outside time, as conceived by traditional aesthetics. That still moment (*Verhoffen*) of animal figure and poem is the moment captured in Rilke's "The Gazelle" (*New Poems*). In "The Meridian," Celan remarks that the poem *verweilt* or *verhofft* at the thought of the "wholly other"; and, further, that no one can say how long the *Verhoffen* or the "breath pause" can last. (*Verweilen* = linger, tarry; it's the verb of Faust's bargain with the devil.) In "The Meridian," Celan himself dwells on the notion of "hope" implicit in verhoffen; in the end, though, a suspensive rendition of *verhoffen* seems better; a hope-ful *Verhoffen* would be quite un-Celanian. The very *ver-* that prefixes *Hoffen* acts like a shadow (of failure, error, loss, breakdown) in advance. The hourglass in the poem perhaps, too, suggests that the gain in sand (silting) issues from a loss of hope: a burial in sand.

Page 26: Behind the charcoal surfaces of sleep

A lyrical interlude amidst the austere poems of *Atemwende*, this poem revisits two of Celan's early poems, "Night Ray" and "Stigma." In the former, the speaker sends his beloved "the coffin of lightest wood. / Waves billow round it as round the bed of our dream in Rome [. . .] A fine boat is that coffin carved in the coppice of feelings" (tr. M. Hamburger). In the latter, the lovers lying in "the clockwork of sorrow" bent "the hands like rods, / and they bolted back and scourged time till blood was drawn" (tr. J. Neugroschel).

Celan interweaves those personal poetic reminiscences with other motifs of his early work: sleep, voyage, alchemy (coal, gold), memory (personal, Romania), history (crematoria). The poem is a parting gesture toward the rich sensuousness of the early work, and even though it reads as another tribute to the surrealist poetics that inspired it (René Char's, among others), Celan's ambivalence vis-à-vis his earlier repertoire is unmistakable. Perfection is of the past tense.

Page 27: Go back and add up

Here and elsewhere Celan's numbers and neologistic numeroids do not necessarily refer to any public convention or private code outside the poem; for example, Twelve-Night is not Twelfth Night. Number and numbered, in Celan, are elements of language; measuring, counting, and numeration are poetic acts as dicey as shooting craps. The orchid (in Greek, testicle) is also known in German as "boy-weed"; in the context of Celan's work as a whole, the orchid participates in a poetic constellation (almond, root, bulb, stone, cloud) that traces the tragic genealogy of the Jewish people. See especially the poem "Radix, Matrix."

Page 28: Half-mauled, mask-

A corbel stone is a stone bracket or supporting architectural member; literally "collar-stone" (which agrees with the other anatomical references in the poem). The poem can be read as a Rilkean gaze into the eye-of-the-beloved, which opens into the strangenesses of a mortuary crypt, and/or as a Rilkean cathedral poem, that is, a response that sees through Rilke's Angel of the Meridian, turning it inside out. Either way, the image exceeds the mind of the imaginer. Finally, talking to stones (Celan's own "Radix, Matrix" begins "as one speaks to the stone") and talking stones (epitaphs) are equally at the origin of poetry—an origin Celan subjects to relentless historical, physiological, and linguistic analysis.

Page 29: From fists white with the truth

Celan's pounded word-walls conflate public wailing-walls with cephalostructures and language centers in the brain.

Page 30: Noisemakers shoot into the light: it's the Truth

The noise maker (*Schwirrholz*) that broaches this poem is an ancient device, used to invoke spirits' voices; in English it's sometimes called "bullroarer," but in English, noise-news (maker) affords an irresistibly Celanian paronymy. (Its poetological significance was noticed by Propertius: "Deficiunt magico torti sub carmine rhombi.")

The uncanny millennarian sheen in the middle stanza issues from a neologism Celan coins out of the word "thousand" in German—no doubt an echo of Hitler's "*tausendjähriges Reich*"; however, in German "thousand" can be used to signify a vague but very large numerical magnitude and hence as a curse word. The menace of large numbers and the hints of ancient and contemporary technology in the poem gave rise to our "macro-mass."

Page 31: You forget you forget

Turning, that is, re-troping, so-called termini technici into metapoetic figures is a move characteristic of Celan's later manner. In this case, earth science, human memory, and poetics are caught in a vortex of metaphors: the poem's point of departure is a literalization (and thus a reversal) of a common process in the history and uses of language: metaphor must "petrify"—be forgotten as metaphor—so it can serve as literal term. Conversely, in the end, all metaphor is consumed and the metaphor of metaphor (which cannot be another metaphor or image) must vanish into the void (if you will, the divine).

In the poem, a piece of once-articulated language (Ger. *Spruch* = saying, dictum, maxim, motto, aphorism, quote from Scripture, proverb, poem, etc.; cp. English- dict-) is defined as *verkieselt*: It has become stone hard through absorption of silica—as in the case of plants and animals buried by volcanic ash: Prevented from decay by the ash, their material combines with silica picked up from the ash by underground water; the result is a semiprecious gem. For Celan, a "technical" description of this sort is nothing other than a description of memory and its response to catastrophic upheaval (with language, the repository of memory).

As a piece of poiesis, this language "fossilized" (or silicified) into "stone" (*Stein*) recalls—with polemic overtones—Heidegger's meditations on Being (*Sein*), Being's forgottenness, and the forgetting of Being's forgottenness. The self-forgetful you, addressed in the poem, should bring to mind Celan's view of poetry as a forgetting of self.

Celan's manuscripts show that the poem evolved around the thought of a "sacrificial bush" (the burning bush, Moses, and the stony tablets of the law). The bush in this case is "diminished" to brush, Ger. *Staude*. (As in the first poem of the collection *Zeitgehöft*, Celan may be thinking, among other things, of the *Wanderstaude*, the tumbleweed or Russian(!) thistle, which breaks away from its roots in fall and is driven by winds.) A burning bush that moves (a footloose fireweed) is a daunting thought indeed.

The poem has been interpreted as memory's passage through a sacrificial fire that makes for deeper forgetting, until the pneuma gathers the speaker in its void (Meinecke). In Celan, though, the memory of burning and the burning of memory are always marked by the irreducibly material historicity of the Holocaust.

Page 32: Crackpots, decomposing

An earlier version of the poem had "mirror" in line 2 which Celan replaced with "depths," perhaps to suggest a breakdown of the mind-mirror analogy and a step beyond the philosophy of reflection it informs. The ghostly-luminous repast of gray may be the reminiscence of a reminiscence of Celan's earlier poem *"Eine Hand."*

Page 33: Lichtenberg's heir-

Woven into the poem are details from G. C. Lichtenberg's life and writings. On 10/4/1790, Lichtenberg wrote to his brother, asking him to keep a special set of tablecloth and napkins in memory of his mother and lost sisters. (The number "twelve" comes from Celan.) In his "secret diary" Lichtenberg mentions a girl who appeared to him as a "white comet," distant, untouchable, and vows to guard the memory of the spot where he observed her first at "meridianal height." "City ramparts" alludes to the topographies of Lichtenberg's memory (of Maria Dorothea Stechard selling flowers to passersby; she died at nineteen).

Research into Celan's sources indicates that he gleaned much of the material from the anthology *German Men* published (under a pseudonym) by Walter Benjamin; Celan may have owned it in the thirties, which (in view of Benjamin's fate) would add a further poignant twist to the poem's acts of commemoration in the face of loss, exile, and language breakdown.

The red "loss of / thought-thread" constitutes a memorable dismemberment of Goethe's image (from *Elective Affinities*): The red thread woven into royal navy cloth (so it can't get lost or misappropriated) becomes, for Goethe, a symbol of the difference that makes a whole cohere and endows it with identity.

Celan's trope of the language towers that are to fall dead-silent contains a translingual crux: In Celan's Russian ear "silent" or "mute" means "German"; for the Slavs, the Germans were the "mute ones," *niemtzy*; during the war and in its aftermath one could often hear the awful paronymy, nazi-niemtzy. Celan's cardinal problem as a poet in German was precisely what he called the German language's "terrifying silence" during the "thousand darknesses of murderous speech" (Bremen-Speech).

Visually (with its slender columnar shape), grammatically (its stack of broken syntax), and thematically (its emphasis on memory, inheritance, affiliation, and transmission), Celan's poem becomes the beacon it calls into being–a tower of language on the verge of silence. We have deliberately foregrounded, in our translation (in other words) the poem's translatorial self-consciousness.

Page 34: The sight of the songbirds at dusk

The "bird" in line 1 is the European blackbird, Ger. *Amsel*, close anagrammatic relative of one of Celan's original names, Antschel/Ancel. (Celan no doubt knew the bird's Latin name, *Mimus polyglottos*—he was a polyglot parrot himself; from the Latin it's a stone's throw to the name of the American mockingbird.) Unlike the New World blackbird, the European blackbird is a songster (just as the mockingbird is). Our version frames the poem in lyric rather than ornithological terms (from "songbirds" to "the singing in our fingers") in order to emphasize the poetological self-reflection but also because the word "black" in the English would contribute a poetically unignorable element that Celan's German does not. The reader sensitive to poetic resonance will notice a deliberate proleptic thickening in our vocabulary choices (e.g., "sight," "ring," and "ungraphed" anticipate "weapons"); in the wake of "weapons," "sight" (in "the sight of weapons") has already lost its scenic innocence. Such thickenings of texture, whenever the target language provides them, are indispensable if one is to do justice to the extraordinarily resonant language of Celan's *oeuvre*.

Page 36: FRANKFURT, SEPTEMBER

"Frankfurt, September" is a study in modern art's origins, means, and ends: On the one side, we encounter the institutions and avatars of culture, interpretation, and commerce (the title points to the international book fair in Frankfurt); on the other, one artist's unsayable pain and privacy.

Freud, who is explicitly named, opens the show as a graven image on a screen and as an apparatus of enlightenment, metonymically displaced by his Cockchafer Dream (a.k.a. the May-beetle dream, analyzed in the chapter on condensation in *The Interpretation of Dreams*). The image of the insect gives us the first hint of Kafka (whose transformed Gregor Samsa is once referred to, erroneously, as a species of beetle). But before we get to Kafka's name, we hear Kafka's voice: "Psychology for the last time" quotes a note of Kafka's, first published with his "Wedding Preparations in the Country" (where, incidentally, a character envies the cockchafer's condition of life). The quote, which serves as a transition from Freud to Kafka, encapsulates Celan's own attitude regarding psychology: He's on record saying psychology neither explains nor excuses anything.

Celan dubs his breakfast eater a *Simili-Dohle*. German *Dohle* (jackdaw) translates Czech *kavka*, from which the name Kafka is derived. Connoisseurs of literary ornitology may recall this diary entry of Kafka's: "In Hebrew my name is Amschel, like my mother's maternal grandfather." Celan's name (before he anagrammatized it into Celan) was Antschel. (He was matrilineally connected with the Jewish community in Bohemia.) The bird in the poem is not the *kavka* itself but a kavka translated into German (the language Kafka wrote in) and a bestsellerized celebrity, to boot: in short, a displaced literary double or semblable—the situation Celan found himself in, too. Insofar as translation is yet another act of doubling and pseudonymyzation, we bared the device by doubling the double. But the fake Kafka is not the end of Kafka. Celan ends his poem by reinscribing the unignorable k's of Kafka's name and literary being into the poem's penultimate word, the **K**ehl**k**opfverschlusslaut, the glottal stop said to be singing—an unheard melody, if ever there was one. In phonetics, glottal stops (or occlusives) are cough-like sounds reconstructed from Proto-Indo-European (the original sounds have been lost). *Kehlkopfverschlusslaut*, the German term for "glottal stop" (lit. occlusion of the head of the throat) is such a throatful that it can choke even a native. Kafka's last days were an agony of emaciation and unsayable pain, his larynx closed by infection. Yet the same closed larynx sang, with mortal humor, in his last masterpiece "Josephine the Singer, or the Mouse Folk."

Page 38: Coincidence staged, the signs all

The curtailed U- at the poem's very center recalls Celan's statement, in "The Meridian," that the poem should conduct its topological quest in the light of U-topia (hyphenation emphasizes the end's no-whereness). Celan's emphasis on u-topia as an *un*-place should be read against utopia *in* place (Nazi, Soviet, or any other). As for this poem, its first four lines sketch a dys-topia in the light of which a utopian place is no longer conceivable even in negative terms, so that what remains is the sheer negativity of the U- (for the reader of philosophical prefixes) or a sheer howl. Many late Celanian poems, from *Fadensonnen* on, are devoted to satirical explorations of the modern dys-topia (these poems were written at the height of the German economic miracle). The apostrophized "Lion" may be Isaac Luria (1534–72), a legendary figure in Jewish mysticism, called Ha-Ari (Ashkenazi Rabbi Isaac), The Lion, author of The Tree of Life (recorded by his disciples).

Page 39: Who

The poem's polemic with color and number, the perceivable and the measurable, calls attention to its quarrel with the traditional means of poetic expression, Celan's own early poetic output included.

The black pennant in the penultimate stanza entropes the poet's sign as a celestial body: A circumpolar star "transiting" the meridian above the pole is in "upper culmination"; the opposite or lowest point is its "lower culmination"; when Venus and Mercury transit across the Sun's disk they appear as dark/black spots against the sun's face. The grotesque figure of the poet as juggler or minstrel appears in several of Celan's poems, and so does the (anarchist) emblem of the black flag. German *Gösch* (small bow-flag) has an etymological history a Celan wouldn't miss: It comes from *Geuse*, which at one time meant a rebel against Spanish rule (in the Netherlands), but in the course of the sixteenth century came to mean "beggar." See also Celan's poem "Shibboleth."

The tunnel shield evoked at the end is a cast-iron cylinder used in large-scale tunneling. Mining, drilling, tunneling—the slow, subterranean groping in the dark toward the You or Thou (as opposed to the unquestioned clarity of garish/false identity)—constitute quintessential acts of negative capability (i.e., poetry) in Celan. (The metapoetic significance of such metaphors goes back to the German romantics, but Celan's frequent use of unpoetic technical vocabularies defamiliarizes the traditional topos.) Tunnel shield in German is *Grabschild*; because the first meaning of *Grab* is "grave," an innocent eye would be tempted to read the word as if it meant a grave plaque—which of course it does, in terms of its larger, poetic sense.

Page 40: Spasms, I love you, psalms

Spasms (*Spasmen*), psalms (*Psalmen*), and semen (*Samen*) constitute an even closer triad in German than in English; the intimacy of creation and procreation in the letter is the genetic mark of the "Jewish strain" (Felstiner's term). In the poem at hand, we have an extreme example of blasphemous but nonetheless sacred revisionism in that the religious bond between psalmist and god is framed as sexual intercourse. For Celan, this act of *oral* intercourse is nothing other than a fundamental ars poetica—just as it was for David (the exultant psalmist's sexual member bears the mark of God). Celan conjoins the second-person pronoun with the image of a narrow chasm (*Du-Schlucht*: note the cavernous assonance) in a figure that can be said to represent the ultimate *Engführung* or straining of language—from speaker to collocutor, from human throat to divine abyss. The pressure exerted upon language in this narrow and perilous passage produces a poetics of paronymy, exemplified here in what may be the quintessential paronymic pair, psalm–spasm. Every item of the original poem has been subjected to this pressure, which drives language beyond language.

It goes without saying that there are more ways than one (and none) to render the vertiginous double chiasmus in the third stanza. In the original Celan plays with the grammatical form "eternal" and "uneternal" both as adjectives (positive and negative) and past participles (from the verb "eternalize" or "eternitize"); in addition, Celan's play generates a host of satellite senses: Starting with 6 (eternal), we get *verewigt*, which means "eternitized" but also "dead," *unewig* ("uneternal"), and *verunewigt*. The last neologism suggests "uneternitized" or, perhaps, de-eternitized. However, insofar as *verewigt* can mean "dead" and *Verewigung* "death," the negative *verunewigt* also conjures up the opposite of "dead,"—a perfectly inextricable tangle of life and death, time and timelessness.

"Red of reds" is a conjectural rendition of Celan's "German" *Rotrot*, based on the form of the Hebrew superlative.

In a "psalm," Celan's *geharft* appears to be related to the psalmist's musical instrument (harp or lyre); hence "strummed" (from the Greek *psalein*, to pluck/twang a stringed instrument). The homonym of *geharft*, meaning screened (or sifted, strained), also makes sense in this context in that it participates in a key Celanian chain of metaphors derived from alchemy: gold–seed/semen–grain, etc.

Page 41: NIGHT IN PAU

Place Royale at Pau contains a famous tortoiseshell that served as cradle for Henry IV; it's inscribed with the dates of his birth and assassination (he was leader of the Huguenots). Zeno of Elea was famous for his refutations of movement (the paradox of the arrow; Achilles and the turtle), which mocked the detractors of his teacher Parmenides. Written during Celan's 1965 "flight" across France, the poem also echoes Valéry's "Graveyard by the Sea" translated by Celan into German.

> Zeno, Zeno, cruel philosopher Zeno,
> Have you then pierced me with your feather arrow
> That hums and flies, yet does not fly? The sounding

Shaft gives me life, the arrow kills. Oh, sun!—
Oh, what a tortoise-shadow to outrun
My soul, Achilles' giant stride left standing.
(tr. C. Day Lewis)

Page 42: LATER IN PAU

Written in Pau in 1965 during Celan's flight, the poem recalls
Celan's 1964 trip to Amsterdam with his wife, whose name (Gisèle
de Lestrange) provides one clue to the apostrophized "stranger."
(See also "Lyon, Les Archers.") While in Amsterdam, Celan had
sought out Spinoza's house only to find a vacant lot. Misunderstood
and accused of "abominable heresy" by orthodox Jews and Chris-
tians alike, Baruch Spinoza was excommunicated by the Jewish
community of Amsterdam and made a living as a lens crafter. The
name Pau, associated with the Albigensian heresy, triggers off the
the thought of Waterlooplein, associated with the Cathar heresy
(both were also known as the Bulgar heresy). Waterlooplein is the
famous flea market of Amsterdam, once called the Jewish Market.

Page 43: The ounce of truth in the depths of delusion

In German only one letter distinguishes delusion (*Wahn*) from the
true or real (*wahr*). The image of the scale occurs in several of
Celan's later poems. In his discussion of the scale-topos in Jewish
mysticism, Gerschom Scholem mentions that it hangs from a place
which doesn't exist and weighs those who do not exist.

Page 44: LYON, LES ARCHERS

In manuscript the poem bears the inscription,

> Lyon 27.10.1965, Cafe Les Archers
> the young girl reading [Camus'] L'Etranger.

Celan was born on November 23, and often uses The Archer (Sagit-
tarius) as an emblem of his star-fated poetic intentions.

Page 46: Attached to out-cast

Morphemically, the German verb *entäussern* expresses a movement
of exteriorization, from inside to outside—which can be looked
upon as relinquishment *or* realization (as in some philosophical jar-
gons). Hence our attempt to slow down the perception of "out-cast"
by means of hyphenation. Aaron's rod (Num. 17.8) budded,
bloomed, and yielded almonds. Has it been crossed here with a
crutch and/or with Mallarmé's flower absent from all bouquets?

The poem's (inverted) crown is, of course, its capitalized No, a
"no" that yields nothing to direct ontological questioning and yet
resonates with distant Celanian "determinations"; for example, his

poem "In Prague" speaks of pure "goldmaker's-No"; in "Speak, you also" the addressee is exhorted not to separate "no" from "yes." In these and other cases Celan demands that we reconsider—if not re-constitute—the grounds of everything we take for granted, that is, for given.

Page 50: Hothouse of an asylum

An earlier version of the last lines had "waving beards" instead of manes of white horses; in one of his Hölderlin poems, "Tübingen, Jänner," Celan writes of the "shining beard of the patriarchs." (German *Schimmel* is etymologically related to "shine" and "shimmer.") The asylum in this poem may bear some relation to Hölderlin's years of incarceration.

Page 51: Lucky, the

Paulownia leaf: see note to "La Contrescarpe."

Page 53: White noises, bundled

Poetry as a message in a bottle is an image Celan associated with Mandelstam.

Page 55: Here are the industrious

Hinging solely on a here (Ger. *hier* has a French shadow, meaning "yesterday"!) that holds language relics haunted by ghosts past and present, the poem is characteristic of Celan's late method in terms of both composition (asyndetic serial notation) and tonality (appre-hensive and satirical, allusive and elusive). It is a poem produced by—and not meant to allay—anxiety. But this anxiety is not of the poet's own psychic state, as some have claimed; rather, it's the anx-iety of memory that revisits places of absence and death, and the anxiety of language at the dreadful end of modernity.

From the very first lines, Celan as a facetious tour guide works with pieces of unsettled and unsettling language. Thus, lines 1–2 in-voke (the cliché of) German industriousness, which, given the country's limited mineral wealth, is a major source of wealth. And yet this boldly trivial distich unmistakably imparts something unsaid and terrible, if the reader chooses to dig under the surface of the in-nocent word *Boden* = "ground," "soil" (the compound *Bodenschatz* = mineral wealth) only to discover to what disturbing uses the virtues of the ground ("soil," "Volk") were put not too long ago; or remem-bers how industry and industriousness—again, not too long ago—were put in the service of extermination. Celan doesn't give prescrip-tions for reading, yet to follow the poem's trails is, invariably, to run into something disturbing or menacing. (For example, "syncope" and Zyklon-B, the cyanide used in the gas chambers, share the same vowels, filtered through very similar consonantal structures.)

The "jubilee year" according to Leviticus 25 would lead to "liberty throughout all the land" as "ye shall return every man unto his possession." (An ironic comment on the German postwar miracle? on God's breach of promise?)

"Spider altars" (*Spinnen-Altäre*): In this conection, the manuscript affords a glimpse into the workings of a poet's mind. Originally, Celan had written *Sinnen-Altäre*, then changed *Sinnen* (senses) to *Spinnen* (spiders). Out of a letter's difference, the poet spins a highly suggestive metaphor much better attuned to the poem's serial menace. In fact, there is a superimposition of two metaphors: The senses spin networks; behind closed doors, the spiders go about their business. The arachnoid, incidentally, is a thin membrane of the brain; the vocabulary of brain anatomy is prominent in the later Celan.

The poem's tour ends in the narrowest place (another act of Engführung!): Celan's *Stehzelle*, cell or stall, may refer to the 3 by 3 arrest cages at Auschwitz, in which a prisoner had room only to stand.

Page 56: When I don't know, when I don't know

The poem seems to have begun as a reminiscence of, or gloss on, Hölderlin: At one point Celan considered Hölderlin's "*Und niemand weiss*" as a possible motto. The words mean "and no one knows" (or, with a different syntax, "and no one can . . ."). In "Rousseau," a poem concerned with orientation during a time of upheaval and with seeing beyond one's own time, Hölderlin remarks, "no one can show you the allotted way [*und niemand / Weiss . . . zu weisen*]; in his "Bread and Wine," no one can tell the whenceness and the whatness of Night's favor; "And no one knows" is also the first line of his "Heimat" (Homeland); the last line of "Der Ister" is similar: "*Weiss niemand*" (nobody knows).

The *Aschrej* prayer is a part of the Jewish service. It comes from the last words of dying Moses, "O happy Israel! Who is like you, a people delivered by the Lord." (Deut. 33.29) Given a poet who thinks in several languages at once, it is impossible not to remember that the Hebrew word *Aschrej* translates (but what can translation mean in this case?!) the German *Heil* (which became the Nazi salute). With one word Celan overturns what the German language knows as *Heilsgeschichte* (the theological interpretation of history that emphasizes God's saving grace). As Jerry Glenn pointed out to us, *Aschrej* can be read as Asch-Schrei (ash-cry or ash-shriek), ironically and literally, depending on the poem's split intra- and interlingual perspective.

The bizarre Hebraization of Pallas Athene performs a similarly unsettling operation: It reminds us, on the one hand, of the Greek utopia German culture dreamed of; on the other, of the unspeak-able experiments that went on in the concentration camps. But in addition to that—and more distressingly—it calls attention to the unbearable German–Jewish tension that informs the poem itself, and to the slippage of Celan's pronominal and national identites (I, you, he, she; Greek, Jewish, French).

Celan's unignorably line-broken "im-mortal" at the end is more than a mere negative acknowledging art's mortality; as with Lucille, in *Danton's Death*, the mortal act of resistance to history—resistance to the point of madness—becomes an act of art.

Page 61: Hush, you hag, and ferry me across the rapids

This disturbing miniature is a rewriting of Celan's early poem "From darkness to darkness" (available in M. Hamburger's selection). Charon, the mythical ferryman of the underworld, has a "staring eye of flame." That Celan deliberately changed the gender of the ferry-man should give pause to any one-sided identification of the femi-nine *Du* figure in his poetry.

Page 62: Eyeshot's island, broken

Here and elsewhere Celan's idiosyncratic compounds (*herzschrift-gekrümelt, Zündschlüsselschimmer*, etc.) pose an intractable problem. In English compounds are a poeticism redolent of the 1890s. Even in German where compounding is a common language pattern, and where there is a tradition of Baroque compounding, Celan's com-pounds are exorbitant; one might even suspect his excesses of vin-dictive intentions. His compounds often destroy reference as such and focus on what makes it possible for language to exceed its in-strumental and/or utilitarian uses. It is, of course, possible to follow Celan to the letter and do excessive compounding in English (we have G. M. Hopkins), but that leads nowhere because translation changes the ground from and against which Celanian compounding derives its power and inventiveness. Compounds thus leave a choice between bad and worse solutions. Most translators (into English and, especially, into French) choose to render Celan's compounds as genitives, such as (the) A of B. We, too, have had to resort to that so-lution more often than we'd like.

The problem is threefold: To begin with, in English the com-pound frequently levels out or parataxizes the relative grammatical values of the two words conjoined, so it's harder than in German in-tuitively to hypotaxize components. Second, despite the flexibility afforded by the genitive in English (conflating the subjective and the objective genitive), the parts of a Celanian compound often do not relate the way tenor and vehicle are supposed to in a genitival

metaphor. To turn a compound into a genitive entails a whole meta-
physics (of unambiguous causation, part/whole disposition, etc.);
yet many Celanian compounds seem designed precisely to obstruct
facile reference and to unsettle any realist metaphysics. Finally, in
the morphology of Celan's poetic manner there is a clear movement
away from analytical genitival metaphors (of the type the-A-of-B),
which are quite frequent in his early work, and toward (synthetic)
compounds (preponderant in the later work). A regular recourse to
analytical genitives would thus distort something very important—
fundamental—in his development as a poet.

Page 63: Eternity gets older: at

Cerveteri, Italy, is an Etruscan archaeological site, and Celan's
poetry constantly revisits sites that bear traces of entire disappeared
peoples.

Page 65: Come, we are cutting out

Rhomboid fossa is the diamond-shaped floor of the fourth ventricle
of the brain—which contains the center of breathing. Its interior
part, shaped like a pen nib, is called the calamus scriptorius. The
poem pushes as far as possible toward what might be called poetry's
neuro-physiological origins. In a characteristic Celanian conflation
of inside and outside moves, the poem is framed as a jaunty excur-
sion to the pond (which is at the same time a kind of surgical ma-
neuver to cut to the quick, in the brain). The whole thing can be
read as a dark comedy: The human mind (craving not only outside
but inside information) remains obscure to itself, has fibers for fin-
gers, and cannot deeply enough name what it turns up from its own
depths, cannot recognize its own cognizances.

Page 67: Soul-blind behind the ashes

Soul-blind (Ger. *Seelenblind*) is the condition of visual agnosia (or
amnesia), the loss or diminution of the ability to interpret sensory
stimuli and thus recognize familiar objects (often as result of brain
damage). Reading Adolf Faller's book on the human body from
which some of the medical terminology in this and other poems is
drawn, Celan underlined the passage that states that the most im-
portant mental functions such as consciousness, intelligence, will,
and memory depend on the intact structure of the pallium or the
mantle of gray matter forming the cerebral cortex. "Visual purple"
(rhodopsin) is the red photosensitive pigment in retinal rods of
fishes and higher vertebrates, which enables them to see in dim
light. It is decomposed by bright light, and must be composed anew
to see in dark. With the evocation of the "sacro-senseless word" (a
reminiscence of Mandelstam's poem "In St. Petersburg," which

Celan translated into German), the poet proposes a sort of neuro-physiological poetics. The "network of vowels" ("pure" voices) seems to conflate, in a complex synesthetic–physiological figure, the inarticulate or, rather, prearticulated voice in the ear's meatus and the image of the eye's retina (etym. "net"). "Networked vowels" suggests—perhaps undecidably—either the latticework of a pure language (we might also recall the absent vowels in Hebrew writing) or language already caught in the eye's net, that is, preformed. The figure of the poet, whose wounded eye/ear can see/hear (in the) voice-inhabited "word-night," is framed by the effort to articulate an ars poetica after the disaster, after everything has been reduced to ashes. The condition of possibility for such a poetics would seem to be a radical inside-out inversion: The footwork is poetological, through a dark (his own?) brain-interior, a space of neuro-physiology, yet already languaged.

Page 70: Out of angel flesh, on

The imagery of this poem is inspired, in part, by Gerschom Scholem's studies in the Kabbalah; see his discussion of the Shekhinah, the phallic tree of the ten Sefirot (numbers or perfections which emanate from God; also, names by which the angels are called), and the hierogamous union of man and woman as an act of ascension that reestablishes primordial oneness. The sister-spouse invoked here recalls figures in the Song of Songs. See also Isaiah 43.5.

Page 72: Walls of speech, space inwards

Celan's neologism *Redewände* recalls the expression "*Wenn die Wände reden könnten*," if walls could speak.

Page 73: Four ells of earth

The original poem is structured by a quintuple anaphora: past participles with the prefix *ver-*. It is also informed by a daring chiasmus that breaks up and then realigns the elements of the catastrophic events in the first and last stanza: Instead of a stone trough (used in bread kneading) and a lightning flash, Celan has a storm trough and a stone flash. The trough or cradle of creation (where "No one kneads us" in Celan's earlier poem "Psalm") thus becomes a figure of universal depression and disaster. Verbal prefixation in English being a much more limited affair than in German, this translation sought to convert the vertical effects (the anaphoric lightning that sparks the poem) into horizontal ones.

In a reading based on Celan's source (Scholem's reconstruction of Kabbalistic creation myths), Pöggeler converts the poem's series of disasters into a final positive useful result (the sun's essence, preserved and purified by the process of fermentation, testifies to the power of tradition to renew itself). But the brain war in heaven responsible for Celan's foul weather won't be stopped by dialectical tricks. Most readers of the original will assume that the figure evoked in the last line, *Hebe*, is the goddess of youth; this makes sense both rhetorically (the evocation of yet a third figure of myth) and psychologically (Celan's wasted youth or *any* wasted youth, all the way back to that of God's first orphan, Adam). It appears, however, that Celan used Scholem's words verbatim and *Hebe* refers to the portion of dough that is the priest's share ("Just as according to the Torah a portion of dough [*eine Teighebe*] is removed from the rest to serve as the priest's share, so is Adam the best share [*die Hebe*] that is taken from the dough of the earth" ("The Idea of the Golem," tr. R. Manheim); Scholem further evokes the legend that God gave Earth a receipt for the "four ells of earth" he borrowed for one thousand years, a receipt kept in the heavenly archives. (Gabriel and Michael witnessed the transaction.) In this scriptural context, Celan's unusual word choice *Hebe* is more than a mere quote from Scholem. It was Luther who first used *Hebe* in the sense of "offering" (as in Levit. 22.12 "the offering of holy things") to designate something not available in the German language. In this sense, Celan's *Hebe* is a transitional aporia: it designates something beyond German, beyond the ashes.

Page 76: As loud colors, heaped up

Ancient belief, mentioned by Scholem, has it that God's eyes have no eyelids: Israel's protector never sleeps. Celan's documented awareness of Scholem's words gives the poem a bitter ironic turn.

Page 79: HAUT MAL

"Haut mal" is the old French designation of epilepsy. (English vocabulary distinguishes between "grand mal" and "petit mal" attacks.) Celan exploits the correlation between this "high" or "divine" malady and the ancient notion of poetic inspiration, and B. Badiou has traced the poem's origin to Celan's reading of Hippocrates:

> I do not believe that the "Sacred Disease" is any more divine or sacred than any other disease [. . .] nevertheless, it has been regarded as a divine visitation by those who, being only human, view it with ignorance and astonishment [. . .]. It is my opinion that those who first called this disease "sacred" were the sort of people we now call witch-doctors, faith-healers, quacks and charlatans. These are exactly the people who pretend to be very pious and to be particularly wise. By invoking a divine element they were able to screen their own failure

to give suitable treatment and so called this a "sacred" malady to conceal their ignorance of its nature. [They picked] their phrases carefully, prescribing purifications and incantations along with abstinence from baths [. . .] their patients were forbidden to wear black because it is a sign of death, to use goat skin blankets or to wear goat skins, nor were they allowed to put one foot on the other or one hand on the other [. . .] none of the inhabitants of the interior of Lybia can possibly be healthy seeing that they sleep on goat skins and eat goat meat [. . .] I believe that human bodies cannot be polluted by a god; the basest object by the most pure [. . .]. Like other diseases it's hereditary. (*Hippocratic Writings*, W. N. Mann tr., pp. 237–240)

From its very title, the poem behaves as a polylogue: *Haut* and *Mal* are common German words (meaning "skin" and "mark," respectively) and, even though their juxtaposition results in a somewhat strained German, the poem that follows this title *is* in German; the combination of *Haut* and *Mal* would recall other formations, such as *Denkmal* (monument) and *Muttermal* (birthmark). So there is almost as much incentive to construe the title in German as in French. The head graphemes seem poised in nearly perfect undecidability. (Consider further the ironic allusion to Ps. 119, "Blessed are the undefiled.")

The figure addressed in the poem—indeed, the figure *of* the poem (subjective and objective genitive)—is gendered feminine in the original. (Gender is ineliminable in the German nominal system.) The reader is invited to decode this Sleeping Beauty's identity at his or her own discretion; we tend to see the figure not as something out there the poem's language refers to, but rather as something that arises out of language and subsumes Celan's poetry as a whole. For example, the literal "your tongue is sooty" invites a bilingual reading because German *russig* (ashen; sooty) is, paronymically, extremely close to *russisch* (Russian), and it was Celan himself who jocoseriously claimed he was a Russian poet exiled among German infidels. "Bilious" in German is designated with the word *gallig*, which suggests Celan's language of domicile, French.

If the poem's head is divided between two languages, its last word is inhabited by two graphemes: German *Glied* (member) contains the grapheme *Lied* (song). In a poem that deserves to be named Celan's Song of Songs (formally, "Haut Mal" resembles the *wasf*, the sequential imagistic description-praise of the beloved's body, as in Song of Solomon 4.1f and 6.14f), this paronymy could hardly be overemphasized. Celan once mentioned that his language was designed and assigned to perform a "spectral analysis of things," to show how they are penetrated by, or fused with, other things. The poet's things, we needn't emphasize, are her words; his words, her things.

Page 80: *The golfball growth*

Pöggeler relates the poem to Leibniz (who suffered from a calcification or growth in the neck and, as a Baroque-age man, wore a full-head hairpiece): Leibniz brought to an end classical metaphysics and inaugurated the calculative technical-scientific thinking of the modern world. The latter, the poem would seem to remind us, cannot reckon (with) death any more than phenomenology can see the back of its head.

Page 81: *Windfield bound for winter: this*

The manuscript contains a note in French: "La où il n'y a pas d'hommes, efforce-toi d'être un homme."

Page 83: *Audio-visual vestiges in*

While this poem no doubt owes something to Celan's experience with mental institutions during the sixties, its vocabulary has a much wider resonance. Celan left Eastern Europe precisely at the time when all educators had to pass through the camps for Marxist–Leninist education, a policy revived during the Cultural Revolution in China. Beyond this historical resonance, the poem's position at the head of his collection *Lichtzwang* suggests a philosophical program on the poet's part, which subsumes the twin coercions of political and psychiatric orthodoxy under the generalized coercive power of a light source or force. The latter tolerates only third-person public functionality, and so subjects the intimate but shifty *you* and its linguistic correlate, poetic speech, to forms of institutional control. We opted for the objective form of the third-person pronoun partly for vernacular naturalness in English and partly to emphasize the third-person's subject–object split.

Page 84: *Knock out*

Words set afloat recur in Celan's poetry as images of his venture into unmapped realms. The first keeper-in-place of poetic language, according to this gnomic poem, is nothing other than light: it is light that drives the wedges which demarcate, differentiate, individuate; thus it is light that *con*fines what it *de*fines and relegates poetic saying to the fixed nomenclatures of history.

Page 85: *Eternities swept*

The evocation of stone and orphans in the third stanza suggests a disjointed pun with far-reaching philosophical implications: German

Waise, orphan, is homophonic with *Weise*, wise man; *Stein der Weisen* is German for the philosopher's stone.

Page 87: Degenerate / Verworfene (2, 290)

Celan's very early sheaf of adages *Gegenlicht* (contre-jour, backlight) shows that his postwar poetic career began with an exploration of contrariety and inversion that led him farther and farther into negativity without return: neither a simple inversion into the opposite, nor a dialectical negation of negation. The end of this poem (a figure of disfigurement? a reminder that poetry produces figures that can't be placed? that out of Auschwitz nothing can be born but abortions?) precludes any final interpretive move.

Klose has established that the goddess in question was probably "inspired" by Fabre's account of the praying mantis; as a "signature of sexuality" (the praying mantis preys, according to the myth, on its male partner) the figure occurs in several of Celan's late poems.

Page 88: Assembly-

It is no accident, perhaps, that Celan's order of poems pairs a failed creation ("Degenerate") with a satire of creation mechanics (in this poem, images of soul-healing are crossed with those of mantid-hatching). Moving from techne's products toward technology's essence, and from visible forms to the fabrication *of* forms of visibility, the poem recalls Celan's suspiciousness of art's points and appointments (voiced in "The Meridian" and elsewhere.)

Page 89: Weather hand

Celan's poetry of nature (to use a misnomer) is poised on the borders of the humanized and humanizable world (glaciers and icefields, tundras and bogs, deserts and mudflats), just as his poetry of language is poised on the borders of signification. In this case, signification is literally bogged down by polysemy and paronymy: German *Lache*, puddle or pool, means also "mark(er)" or "tapping" (secreting resin); in this paludial land/skull-scape *Lache* won't fail to conjure up *Leiche*, corpse. Celan's interest in bogs—one he shares with the Irish poet Seamus Heaney—is related in part to the capacity of bogs as uncanny natural memory, preserving bodies undecomposed. Our version highlights Celan's interest in sound intricacies, punning and paronymy (e.g. puddle-paludal-pedal). "Weather hand" recalls the English "weather eye."

Page 91: We always find ourselves

The initial poem in Celan's collection *Schneepart*, "We always find ourselves" is a poetic colon of sorts, a gathering up of motifs and near self-citations from earlier poems (in particular, this poem can be read as a rewriting of the initial poem in *Die Niemandsrose:* see

Hamburger's translation of "There was earth in them") and a launching into new, ever colder—and stranger—latitudes.

Page 92: Lilac twilight daubed with yellow windows

The occasion of this poem was a winter-night walk during Celan's first and last postwar visit to Berlin in 1967—an occasion supercharged with personal and historical memory (hence the extreme economy and compression of reference and allusion). The beginning is innocently picturesque: Berlin's "lilac twilight" is the city's artistic signature—a commonplace in post-symbolist art and poetry; with the evocation of "yellow" blotches, however, the cityscape begins to lose its innocence, especially in apposition to Jacob's Staff (the stars of Orion that dominate the winter sky). The constellation shines over the rubble of what until the war was Berlin's Anhalter Terminus, one of the architectural glories of an imperial city. In the backlight of the stars, the picturesque yellows recall, inevitably, the yellow Jewish stars now vanished from Berlin. It's no accident that Celan led his friends (and the reader) to that place: It's the place of his first arrival in Berlin, at the time of Kristallnacht (see "La Contrescarpe"). The station's "rubble" in this case is designated with a non-Berliner word, betraying a viewpoint that is both foreign (Austrian) and pejorative. (The word used to mean "fragment"or "lump," until an eighteenth-century translator of Milton used it in the plural to coin a neologism that now means "ruins.") The next stanza, however, takes us back to Berlin, linguistically, with the street-talkish Kokelstunde, the hour of matchsticks or of "playing with fire." The image thus compresses a sarcastic evocation of small-street sentimentality and big-time arson (from Kristallnacht to World War II). Thereupon Celan again changes the linguistic key, using a Latin-based neologism with an all-European resonance, *Interkurrierendes:* This momentary (?) absence of an "intercurrent" event can be read—notice Celan's signature, the menacing ambiguity—as one turning the picturesque cityscape into a veil of history (no one to start a fire this time, yet the ruins remain). At the end, the topos of snow (silence, oblivion, etc.) casts its pall on the scene, while a pun hinged on a single sound (*Steh-* vs. *Schnee-*) shifts the perspective from the neighborhood tavern to the chambers of snow—the last end of those who gathered at taverns to boost their spirits before Kristallnacht.

Page 93: You with the dark slingshot

A Goliath's apostrophe to David's God.

Page 96: The aural apparatus drives a flower

An ironic allusion to Rilke's first sonnet to Orpheus? We didn't mean to force a green fuse on the line—nor do we refuse a good allusion's force.

Page 97: Open glottis, air flow

(Human) vowels always have more than one formant (G.-M. Schulz). Traditional philosophy, based on the the metaphysics of voice, regards vowels as the medium of spirit; consonants, as the obstruction of matter. With its hint of deficiency in vowel quality and spirit, this poem would seem to suggest a mode of "articulation" on the borderline between animal voice and machine noise. (The vowels of God's name are not to be spoken.)

Page 98: Raised bog, in the shape of

The English nomenclature of bogs distinguishes between "raised bogs" and "blanket bogs." The former are sometimes described as "domed" since the turf grows above the water level; in German, the same visual logic results in the name *Hochmoor* ("highmoor") which is said to have a watch-crystal shape. Celan, characteristically, literalizes the standard German descriptive metaphor and moves from the timepiece's outside (the crystal) to the very mechanism of time indication and thus from human (clockwork) time to geological time. As a result, it becomes impossible to tell temporal (or the metaphorical) from spatial (the literal) landscape, indication from figuration, justice from ingestion.

Sundews are carnivorous bog-dwelling plants, secreting from their leaves a dew-like viscid substance, digesting the trapped insects, and expelling the skeletal remains. As the swallowtail (butterfly) is called *Ritter* (knight) in German, the line reads like an entomological version of *La Belle Dame sans Merci*. In the original, the candle-like mullein flowers are called Sabbath candles, which, in turn, are associated with the arrival of the zaddik and with a breakaway from clockwork temporality.

Page 99: Particles, patriarchs, buried

The glitter of buried ore (precious metal) and the panonymic nuggets (*Erzflitter–Erzväter; Kalkspur–Karstwannen–Kargheit–Klarheit*) are conjoined, geo-poetologically. Angiosperms are vascular plants (roses, orchids); they have their seeds in a closed ovary. The end of the poem uses the karst formations in Romania as figures of poetic self-reflection.

Page 100: And force and pain

The end of the poem recalls the Yiddish song (used by Celan as an epigraph for "Benedicta") in which a man goes to heaven to ask God if things ought to be the way they are.

Page 101: A reading branch, just one

One of the longest and most difficult among Celan's later poems, "A reading branch" anatomizes the process of reading and the emergence of poetry as a counterstatement to contemporary news reports. Starting with what seems to be a medical probe or brain scan, and alluding to the physiology of visual perception, the poem probes the parallel universes of outer space and inner brain, confrontation and solidarity. Its bifurcated structure (two symmetrical parts, each 17 lines long) mimics the structure of the optical chiasma, the branching and crossing of the optical nerves. After a series of polarities (left and right eye, right and left hemisphere of the brain, space probe and bloodclot, land and sea, terrestrial (human) and lunar (inhuman) landscapes, lit and dark side of the moon), the name of Pilsen (line 24) signals a switch to the political polarity of East and West in the late 1960s and the Warsaw Pact invasion of Czechoslovakia (the "landlocked" country alluded to in line 16). In manuscript, the poem is dated August 21/22, 1968, precisely the night after the invasion. Its immediate occasion thus seems to be the coincidence of private and public forms of incursion, excursion, and the crossing, in the reader's mind, of two textual universes: news reports of the progress of the U.S. Apollo Program (Celan was keenly interested in the opening up of new realms and the historical and human consequences of conquest, see "The Syllable Pain") and news reports of the Soviet-led invasion of its unruly satellite nation. (In a poem written on the day of the invasion, Celan recapitulated the event with two letters: ZK. In East-German German, the initials ZK stood for *Zentralkomitee*; their mirror image, KZ, stands for *Konzentrazionslager*.)

Our version follows readings by Speier and Zschachlitz, but many elements of the original remain conjectural.

Page 103: The cables have already been laid

In its deliberately mixed diction (militarese, legalese, health-and-fitness-ese), this poem seems remarkably prescient of the pathology of promissory discourses in commerce, in our time.

Page 104: Nowhere, with its silken veil

The poem revisits the connection between nowhere and daylight (associated with boundaries, separation, loss), superimposing several frames of metaphor—inside a medical insititution, inside the apparatuses of time and language, inside (and outside) being. Hence the hint of transcendental tele-phony, between the ontologically separate self and other. Poetry promises the giving of being to (and through) the other, but ordinary language (in this instance its pro-nominal system) resists the rearticulation of that relationship; hence the strangeness of the last lines. (This strangeness has inspired the notion that the poem reads in German as if it were (already) a trans-lation from the Hebrew, not only in terms of echoes and allusions but in terms of its very grammar (Stadler). Such an exposure of the lyric genre to several thousand years of translatorial history across several languages (sacred and profane) proposes unfathomable depths. Cf. Felstiner's "Translating Paul Celan's 'Du sei wie du.'")

Page 105: In the most remote of

Starting with the "stairway of amens," several details in the poem al-lude to Jacob's dream of the ladder in Genesis 28 and beyond it to the steps of the Temple in Jerusalem (as the end of the pilgrimage). With its displacement of paralysis, from human body to sacred ground, the poem questions the ability of secular humanity (Dasein) to overcome its crisis of faith and climb into the holy; it also calls into question its own language: The scale of paralyzed affirmations is preceded by a scale of meaning, with Dasein being at the farthest remove from meaning. The word "Supernothing" was coined by the sixteenth-century mystic Angelus Silesius. Celan's studies in nega-tive theology have left many traces in his poetry.

Page 107: O little root of a dream

Metaphors of digging, mining, excavating, rooting, etc. are common in Celan's poetry and invariably have a self-reflexive linguistic di-mension. In German, the earth-language connection rests on a pow-erful anagram: *Rede* (speech)–*Erde* (earth). Mud was always in the mouth.

In German, *vom Blatt singen/lesen* (lit. read from the sheet) means "to sight-read." Celan inverts the expression by adding "blind" to the sheet/leaf (*Blindblatt*). Interestingly, the sheet/leaf remains invisible (or blind) in the meaning of the idiom. The ambi-guity of "you read me blind" is an attempt to suggest the self-effacing quality of the original language.

Page 108: Don't sign your name

This poem was published posthumously in Paul Celan, *Eingedunkelt und Gedichte aus dem Umkreis von Eingedunkelt*, Hrsg. von Bertrand Badiou und Jean-Claude Rambach. Suhrkamp: Frankfurt, 1991.

INDEX OF
ENGLISH TITLES / FIRST LINES AND
GERMAN TITLES / HALF TITLES

Numbers in parentheses refer to volume and page number in Paul Celan, Gesammelte Werke, Suhrkamp Verlag, 1983.

about the author

PAUL CELAN is widely considered to be the greatest postwar German poet. Born Paul Antschel in 1920 in Czernowitz (then part of Romania, today in Ukraine), he lived in France from 1948 until his death in 1970. Among the translations of his work into English are *Last Poems* (edited, selected, and translated by K. Washburn and M. Guillemin), *Poems of Paul Celan* (edited, selected, and translated by M. Hamburger) and *Speech-Grille and Selected Poems* (translated by J. Neugroschel).

about the translators

NIKOLAI POPOV teaches English and Comparative Literature at the University of Washington in Seattle. A James Joyce scholar and translator, he co-translated with Heather McHugh a collection of the poems of Blaga Dimitrova, *Because the Sea Is Black* (Wesleyan, 1989).

HEATHER MCHUGH is Milliman Distinguished Writer-in-Residence at the University of Washington. In addition to six acclaimed books of poetry and the collection of essays *Broken English: Poetry and Partiality* (Wesleyan, 1994) she has translated poems by Jean Follain and Euripides' *Cyclops*.

Library of Congress Cataloging-in-Publication Data
Celan, Paul.
    [Poems. English. Selections]
    Glottal stop : 101 poems by Paul Celan ; translated by Nikolai Popov and Heather McHugh.
        p.   cm. — (Wesleyan poetry)
Poems originally published in German in the author's Gesammelte Werke or in Eingedunkelt und Gedichte aus dem Umkreis von Eingedunkelt. Frankfurt-am-Main : Suhrkamp Verlag, 1983, 1991.
Includes index.
    ISBN 0-8195-6448-6 (alk. paper)
    1. Celan, Paul—Translations into English. I. Popov, Nikolai B. II. McHugh, Heather, 1948-   . III. Title. IV. Series.
PT2605.E4 A25 2000
831'.914—dc21   00-009307